Manifestations

ELAINE RAGLIN

Table of Contents

Preface

It hit me like a ton of bricks when I realized that I had penned one of the most controversial books that ever hit the shelves. Had I been totally honest while writing the book, I probably would not have seen tomorrow. Yes, I am saying that I am a product of an environment that somehow adopted the philosophy that if you shoot, you'd better shoot straight! 'Shoot straight' encompasses all areas: physical, mental, emotional. I am a Raglin, and I have the Raglin philosophy buried deeply within.

I have pondered the notion for years whether I should pen this book for my twin sons, Justin Ryan Raglin and Austin Bryan Raglin seeing that I was about forty years old when I birthed them. Over time, I realized that they knew very little about me and how I grew up. At this stage of the game, I wonder if finding out even matters to my beloved. However, the past is the past, yet it has a purpose. If we forget our past, we might repeat it based on genes, blessings, curses and culture. We need to know our past in order to avoid the bad and to embrace the good in the present. There's not a lot that was left out of this testimony. However, some areas could be highlighted in more detail, which could have caused me to pen another book immediately. And some areas might need to be discarded altogether. Nevertheless, here she is my life as I want the reader to see it.

My lifestyle had to change drastically when I birthed twins. So, they would not really know me because before their arrival I was a totally different than the person that I am today. Before their births, my life was all about me. Now I had to experience a paradigm shift. My life was now all about them. I would become a 'Mother of Twins' (M.O.T.). I would join the M.O.T. Group and learned to answer to my new name, 'Twins' Mom'. Not only was I forced to answer to the name, 'Twins' Mom' in the group, I had to respond in kind at daycare, at school, at church in Boy Scout Events, karate practice and practically wherever I went. I felt a sense of shock when people called me by my name at the few social events that I attended without them. These guys really dominated my life. I did not know what it was to go to the drive-thru and buy one sandwich. I always purchased three or more. The only time that I purchased one was after I had been to one drive-thru and one of the twins decided that he did not want what the other two of us were eating. Dumb me would drive to another drive-thru to appease the other. Now, when I reflect, I was too tired to fight. It was easier for me to succumb to the whining and rush home to get started on preparations for the next drooling day.

I worked and drove them to school most of their elementary school and junior high school days. I would then pick them up after school and drive them to their after-school Latchkey Programs and rush back to my job to finish the day. I was operating on autopilot.

I think that the worst thing that can happen as the result of my penning the book is that the reader views childbirth outside marriage in a negative light. I can say that everything that took place from getting pregnant with the twins to single parenting them until I was satisfied that they were men was to say the least, phenomenal. There are so many different facets to this subject of reproduction that I dare not attempt to exhaust the list in this book.

However, I personally think that most pregnancies are unplanned, and accidental because the sexual partners are merely relieving their biological urges and their uncontrollable passions. I have also come to know that in the game of life various relationships are formed for selfish reasons, reasons having nothing to do with procreation. Procreation in these instances just happens to be a byproduct of the sexual act, which take place while powerplay and true passion is taking place. In other words, relationships are rarely formed for the purpose of procreation. While this is not an area to be judgmental about, as no one really knows what God's Plan is. If I may share my opinion, I think that more babies are conceived out of powerplay than out of true love. Yet once those babies are born, the mother has a stronger bond than that of the father. The mother dotes over the baby, pampers her and grooms her for independence.

God is in control of life and death. And I out of reverence for God, am not to judge what the circumstances are at the time of conception nor whether God should have allowed the pregnancy to come to term because conception took place between a man and a woman, who were not married in the conventional style.

I thank God that I was able to stay focused and was able to move forward with my life as a single parent. I realize that while it is not viewed as popular in society's view, there are some advantages to single parenting. Single parenting prevents the complications of a tug of war between the two parents when there is difference in opinion about what should be done about matters that come up regarding permissions allowed the child(ren). I was in power and had all authority. I was happy when things went well and had the sole responsibility when things went awry. I did not have to consult anyone other than God when things went awry.

I thank you, my sons, for cooperating with me, which helped me to heal after having had such a difficult time forgiving my Mama for leaving me at an early age of three and Daddy's untimely death as I was approaching age 12. Each of you have contributed to my self – image in ways that I never would have imagined. Your father tried to take the credit from God. He told me that had he not impregnated me, I would have become a bum. And I do have to admit that he did me a favor. I say this because there was no time to be a bum.

When the twins arrived, it was no longer about me. I was forced to adjust my attitude about life, buckle down and acknowledge that it was about them. And there are no regrets that I was entrusted by God to have them. I resolved those children are gifts. And God always gives good gifts.

I also have a disclaimer. It is my prayer that the reader of the book does not take anything personal that is mentioned in its contents. I merely wanted to make the book about my life and struggles with forming a palatable self-image of myself. If the reader is in the characters in the book, I have omitted names to protect the reader from unsavory attacks from others, who do not know my story. If the character receives notoriety from others who have read my story, I am willing to share the glory.

I thought in depth and questioned the need to change the me that I was before I experienced childbirth but was never quite able to figure out what I needed to change about myself to be a good parent. I certainly had not figured my problem to be self-centeredness. This was all to change once I moved to St. Louis, Missouri where I was to find my answer in quite an unorthodox manner.

I had heard that having kids requires one either to work harder, or to win the Lottery. Neither of these options are easy. I was required to work harder, and I still aspire to win the Lottery. Winning the Lottery would be a Blessing. I would put the money to good use by helping myself, my sons and special causes to help others become more spiritually mature. I admit that I am allergic to hard work. The money would have to work for me to accomplish my vision. This I do know; my sons did not get their love for hard work from me.

Sometimes I was so exhausted that I would let my kids get away with things they should have been punished for. And on other times, I gambled on the belief that a child could be raised by the parent letting her know that the parent trusted her to have good behavior, the child would reward the parent by showing good behavior. That is the way I grew up. This was my default system. So, I gambled with raising my sons this way. It was out of necessity that I tried the technique. And I won. My sons were on good behavior until they left the nest.

However, I was not looking at the principle at the time that I was doing it in a philosophical manner. I was looking at the principle from the perspective that if I did not do it the way I had reasoned, I would not have been able to bring my children up in a manner that they would be a contribution to society. And I would not have survived the stress of figuring out how to make the parts of the puzzle fit. I had not done this style of living before. I was a single parent. Since being a success is what I was determined to do, this survival tactic was as if I had gone to Las Vegas, NV and hit the jackpot!

Parenting when one is as far along as I was in life was challenging. I had not practiced. I did, however, learn a few things along the way as I started working with children in my career around the time that my sons were toddlers. While I learned that there is no one best way to parent, I found that there were about four different ways by using best practices of childrearing as tested by the profession. I also tested some of them and was convinced that authoritarian parenting, while risky has its benefits. Authoritative parenting has been found to have the most effective results in all sorts of ways for my family: academic, social emotional, and behavioral. As an authoritative parent, I expected a lot from my children, but in turn, I had to expect even more from my own behavior. There could not be any deviation from the driven path. 'Don't do as I do, do as I say do' did not work here. As the authoritative parent cannot do anything that they do not want the child to do in the child's presence nor to the child's knowledge. Frankly, I did not do anything to contradict my teaching because I was too tired to deviate from the schedule and the driven path. Once we ended our days with the many activities completed, we all were too tired to do anything besides go to bed.

This is not to say that there were not risky times occasionally. You see, I had not considered the fact that I was raising revolutionists. These boys were of the generation where what I was taught and was doing was obsolete. The teachers were influencing and teaching them a new way. I was appalled to learn that one of Austin's elementary teachers allowed him to write an essay titled "All About Me." I thought the title of the essay was egotistical. Austin embraced the thinking 'It's all about me', and I was challenged to ensure that he did not go through life with the attitude that life was all about him.

I did not learn until they were in middle school that the teachers did not teach them cursive writing. I remember their telling me that the teachers told them that they did not need to know how to read and write cursive. I thought they were being untruthful. Oftentimes, they told me that they could not read my handwriting. I write in cursive. I think that printing by hand is too slow. They print. They tried to write in cursive, but one's looked like little beads on paper and the other's was like a doctor's handwriting. I lost the battle.

I also lost the battle of getting Justin to turn his homework in to the teacher. We had worked very hard on the homework. I even started penning the homework on the back of his jacket and it still would not make it to the teacher. I stopped trying to help with their homework when they were in the fourth grade. They had New Math. Math was my weakest subject. The coursework was so difficult for me that I felt that I was retarded. I gave up. They started telling me that they were not turning the work in because the answers were incorrect. I became wiser and enrolled them in an afterschool tutoring program.

Austin, I will not forget, yet I forgave you for calling the police on me at 3 am because you learned in daycare at age four that you should call 911 if you were left home alone and if someone touched you inappropriately. Austin man, your timing and your judgment were offkey that time. I had no idea you were calling the police to test your knowledge and skill of dialing 911 when I saw you get out of the waterbed with your brother and me to make your historical call. You then got back into bed to wait for the police, I suppose. They did come. One officer was banging on the backdoor and another on the front. The officer reached for his gun when I answered the front door looking unruly with blond hair standing straight up on my head. He said in a stammer, "We got a call from this address by a child saying he was left home alone." Thank God, they accepted my statement. I was convincing probably because of my groggy, unruly appearance and my pajamas.

As Justin was not to be outdone, about two weeks later, he called 'Officer Black', my police officer name for getting all the neighboring children to behave correctly. They all knew there were police officers at the headquarters one block away. There were about eleven of them on the block, a Cul de sac.

One day Mama was visiting. I was doing her hair with the front door open to catch a breeze when a tall police officer stepped into the doorway. Justin was sitting in the middle of the sofa with his hands crossed and his legs crossed. I noted that this was an unusual pose. I noticed right away that Justin had pulled a stunt. I told the police officer, "Yes, I already know officer that you got a call saying that a kid was home alone." The officer told Justin not to do that because the police would think the next call was a prank when the police would truly be needed. Both of you were convinced that the police would come if you called them.

Those teenage years were the greatest challenge for me. The hormones shifted and you boys were stepping out on your own. You were no longer listening to me. I was having my own problems. I was going through a storm and a crossroad in my life at that time. I saw that there was a need for a change in my parenting style to a more permissive model. I needed a break. And with this style, I thought it more age-appropriate for boys. The twins were now free to try their own wings on some things. They were free to walk a block to Boy Scouts, visit friends if I knew their parents, and go to Summer Camp when the grades were up to par. They were getting ready to start driving. I think that they enjoyed driving more when they did not have a permit or a driver's license than they do now. Parents, I highly recommend against teaching the child to drive yourself. Send them to Driver's School! When I took on this chore, I thought that I would surely have a heart attack. I am not sure of what I was thinking. It certainly was not logical. One of the twins would drive too fast and the other would drive too slow on the highway. It was about this time that I was diagnosed with hypertension.

Working and going back to school at 52 years old was very stressful. Twins, you did not complain openly about that, and I highly appreciate your allowing me to pursue my dreams. The Master of Social Work Degree from Washington University was quite an accomplishment. The students loved you and thought that you were cute. You were on such good behavior that they did not mind buying your dinners. Obviously, you were night owls, like me. Washington University likes its groups. All of us students worked days. We had to meet at night. Thank you for your support.

Austin, I did not believe you when you said that you were going to the Army because you used to fear everything. You played all the time. Thank God that he provided age-appropriate toys for you. I have no idea what you might have created had you come up as I had, playing with my imagination. I would take a corncob and imagine that it was a girl whose hair was the corn shuck. I would comb the corn shuck until it began to look like a fine hair strand. I would then braid or curl the combed corn shuck and make it look like a hairstyle. Little did I know that there was a true artist lurking within you.

Justin and Austin, you had rollerblades. I had roller skates. I went skinny dipping in the family pond. You went kayaking in a swimming pool at the Boy's Club. The differences in our worlds were phenomenal. I grew up in the country on a farm. You grew up in the city. In many ways I think that growing up in the country was better than growing up in the city for kids.

Austin, the Boy Scouts really paid off for you. I could see the man kicking in when you became an Eagle Scout and went away to the Pre-College Summer Programs. I am proud of your accomplishments. And thank you for your service in the Army. Eagle Scouts got you bumped up a notch there. Osama Bin Laden was not one of my favorite people. I fell short on loving this enemy. But did you have to go to Afghanistan twice? I was wondering what I would do had you brought an Afghan bride home to St. Louis. Thank you for choosing someone who speaks English fluently.

Justin, you were the one who always took risks and liked to be in charge. You would take liberties without telling me. You thought it only natural for you to take the extra car to go visit your girlfriend across town without a permit or a license. One time you decided that you wanted to visit a friend after school, who lived miles away. When the friend's father picked him up from school, you got in the car too. I could not believe that you thought that you would have that liberty. I became very upset and had to call the parents and let them know that you were away from home without permission. They graciously returned you to me at once. Then, I learned that you were working in high school, and I did not even know it. I thought that was strange but felt better about it once I learned that it was part of your curriculum for graduation. I was in for an education when I learned that from henceforth, high schoolteachers do not communicate with parents more than twice a year by appointment only. I was later to learn that college teachers do not communicate with parents at all. They just seem to want the parents to pay tuition. The student would have to commit a crime before the school calls the parents. Thank God you did not do that.

However, Justin, you liked to daydream and would often be in the clouds when I needed an immediate response from you. Daydreaming must have been one of your defense mechanisms to keep me at bay.

Justin, I struggled with keeping you from becoming an old man too soon. I am a firm believer that, if possible, a child should be a child until it is time to leave the nest. I apologize for leaning on you and Austin so heavily sometimes; but your judgments were so pristine. Or should I say that most of the time, your judgments on the big things were pristine. I trusted you and depended on you to do the right things.

Justin, you have always had a way of thinking things and not telling anybody what you are thinking. Despite your caretaker personality, I really like your ability to influence and charm others. Did you really read all those Harry Potter Books? Thank both of you for being there. Live your lives.

Hopefully this work will help you sons to know more about your ancestry on my side of the family and how I was brought up. I also hope that you will not wait too long before you find your peace and your best selves. I pray dear children that you will step out on faith and listen as God to shows you your purposes. "Wait on the Lord, I say Wait on the Lord."

I was not born with a silver spoon in my mouth, yet I had opportunities that many others would die trying to get. And then I know that I have had many haters all of my life. This lets me know that I have had favor all my life and that I continue to have favor. I have oftentimes failed to realize that I did not have to be so Blessed. Many times, I failed to give God the glory that He so rightfully deserves. I wonder why people refer to God 'the higher power' as 'the man up above', and other names that do not measure up anywhere close to who He is. "He is God!" If there is a way to coin in one word how to describe God, I wonder what it would be. 'God is' is two words.

My sons, when I was growing up, there was no questioning what the grownups were doing. And there was no questioning how things had happened to make history as it is now. Children did not get involved in adult conversation. Children stayed in their places. When adults were talking children were expected to leave their presence.

When I was growing up, there were no cell phones, printers, Computers, laptops, color television, Internet, Wi-Fi. Or any of the conveniences that we have now in this information age. Hard work was the norm. If there was a telephone, it most likely would have a party line. On the Party Line, you can hear what your neighbors are saying If you picked up your phone to dial someone. If you wanted to be rude and impolite, you could listen in on their entire conversation without their knowledge. This type of technology could very well have broken up families. Luckily the spouse was usually away from home trying to make a living. Therefore, any gossip would have been transferred by the person who had been eves – dropping on another's conversation. I am pretty sure the police still use them. Years ago, I was on the phone at work one day in a high crime neighborhood and learned that I was not the only person on the phone. Two men were talking. When I asked them to clear the line, I was screamed at and told that I needed to give up the line and they kept talking. Being shocked by the response, I hung up. I was shocked to learn that there are still party lines in the crime ridden areas of the city.

Because there were no printing machines, duplicate copies were made with carbon paper. Usually, one could not do more than 3 carbons at one time. Can you believe that the City of St. Louis still uses carbon paper to make copies in 2021? This fact was shared by Former City Treasurer,

Tishaura Jones during her campaign debate for mayor. Ballpoint pens came along shortly after I was in Junior High. We thought it stylish to be able to write with the fountain pen. It reminded me of George Washington and the founding fathers writing and signing the Constitution. However, use of the pen is a slow process.

When I was growing up, before children were off to school the animals on the farm had to be fed and the cows milked. There was no pasteurized milk back then. The milk would have to be used right away to prevent the milk from becoming sour, which was not something you wanted to use in your cakes and other desserts. The children churned the milk from the cows and made homemade butter. It was a process because the milk had to become sour and clabber, like jelly, then churned until the curds were beaten into buttermilk. The butter would rise to the top of the churn, be removed and placed in a container. It was delicious! While I still eat cornbread and buttermilk occasionally, it does not taste quite the same. The pasteurized buttermilk that we use today does not taste the same.

When children came home from school back then, they quickly changed their clothes and were off to the cotton field to either chop cotton or to pick cotton. There was very little time for homework. The children were then off to bed to get up early the next day and start the routine all over again. This is just a little of the difference between how you and I were raised. Admittedly, I was exempted from much of this kind of work because by the time I was work ready, Daddy no longer had a farm. However, we continued to live in the farmhouse.

My sons, if I had any worthwhile advice to give you, I would say, "You've got to give the kind of love you want to get." Afterall, you reap what you sow. In agriculture terminology, if you plant apples, you do not reap oranges. I also would like to share with you that a true friend is anyone who will help you get to your destiny. A true friend many times have to muster up and tell you what you do not want to hear, the truth.

Sons, if you obey God, you will never have a bad memory. I say just obey. God has laws. These laws are not explained they are just announced, and you must obey whatever He says do. Do not test the manufacturer's laws by trying something that you think is better. God is the manufacturer. He made us and not we ourselves. Laws of any kind are not to be broken. I learned more about the consequences of breaking the laws of chemistry when I broke them trying to give myself a cold wave after having had a relaxer when styling my hair. I had broken the bonds in my hair shaft with the relaxer, so the hair would not curl after going through the tedious task of getting the cold wave. The choice was a wig or a bald haircut, both of which I disliked. And, oh yes, Oil and water do not mix. 'I know you get my drift.' Keep the two separated.

I have the sweetest and kindest sisters and nieces and nephews that one could ever wish for. Many of them helped keep me straight on the facts in this novel. To Martha Jean, Stellarine, Hattie Mae and Selma, thank you for laboring with me to get this book to the place where anyone would like to read it.

I also would like to thank other writers for sharing with me about how the self – publishing industry works. I learned a lot. It motivated me to move forward with my writing. I truly enjoyed writing this novel.

I must give the reader the task of figuring out who the actual characters are in this story. You did not think that I would do all the work on my own, did you? This book spans over a period of approximately half a century. I expect the second volume to be even more of a thriller. The second period entails my experience of single parenting. Oh boy, was I to learn a lot from that experience. I am so glad that I had this experience. The good outweighed the bad.

I have learned to walk in my truth and finally to use the Word of God to order my steps. I seek His Counsel more often, now. To God be the glory for all the great things that he has done and continues to do in my life. I cannot wait to learn all His promises.

My journey in life has not been a clear-cut path by any means. In the back of my mind, I have always had a certain feeling of insecurity as to whether where I am is where I need to be. But I have watched God's hand lead me to green pastures, having nothing to do with my ability or effort on my part. Amazingly, He has closed doors and opened new ones repeatedly as He sees fit. Most times, I am unaware of what He is doing. Nevertheless, He does it and I have to thank Him for always doing the right thing for me.

God placed me under good Spiritual Leadership. And I have been nourished and fed the Word of God as never before. For approximately twenty years, I have been under the leadership of Bishop Steven G. Thompson and his Helpmate Supreme Elect Lady Merlean Thompson in St. Louis, Missouri. I have grown as I watched them grow in faith. I thank God for having leaders who unselfishly imparts the Word of God and does not hesitate to give God the glory.

MANIFESTATIONS

Honor Your Mother and Your Father

Like most others, I was born not having any idea of my purpose. Nor had I spent a lot of time thinking about my purpose until I became much older. I say that I was older because most of us do not know our purpose because our parents, unlike the parents of Samson, whose parents told him that he was a Nazarite, nor like Jesus, whose parents knew that He was to be the Savior of the World and John the Baptist, whose parents knew that He was the forerunner of Jesus, the Christ, our parents had not told us that we had a divine purpose. Those parents who do not know are most likely preoccupied with their own situations and circumstances and childbirth was just another of those situations and circumstances blended into their current situations.

After reading the Book of Genesis in the Holy Bible years later in life, it was revealed to me that all mankind is assigned a divine purpose when God decides to make Himself a man. That divine purpose is for man to act like God on this Earth, subduing the Earth and exercising dominion and exercising the Will of God on Earth. I now understand that we are to make the Earth a Garden of Eden. I have come to know that we are to put our God-given bodies, spirit, gifts and talents together and make good things happen in this earth. These good things range from natural to supernatural. The natural would incorporate all physical things and the supernatural all spiritual things. God being spirit, does not need a body. Therefore, when man communicates with God, he must communicate on a spiritual level.

I understand that God gave man dominion over the earth after Adam and Eve were evicted from the Garden of Eden, God's Paradise. Adam being given everything in Paradise, did not appreciate what God had done for him. Adam disobeyed God and was now to work in the earth and duplicate the Paradise that he had been evicted from.

Adam's DNA, tarnished by the sin that he committed in the garden is now passed on to his offspring, who must work in the earth. Adam's off-spring, tarnished by the original sin committed in the Garden of Eden have the responsibility to assist in God's Divine Plan as witnesses. Each offspring has his own assignment from God, the Father and man must be obedient to God's instruction and live or face spiritual death and oftentimes physical death as the result of being disobedient. Bible Study has taught me that there is even a second death, the one that one should avoid, "by any means necessary." This is the death that one experiences when his name is not in the 'Lamb's Book of Life, 'according to John in the Biblical Book, 'The Revelation'.

I had to decide what I was willing to do to accomplish getting this novel published. I would fly high. I could not say it any better than the famous Pastor Dale Bronner, "Whenever you fly high, some crows will jump on your back. The eagle just flies higher until the crows cannot tolerate his altitude. The crow's oxygen gets cut off. The crows then must jump off the eagle's back to survive."

Remember the words of the prophet Isaiah in Chapter 40, verse 31 "They that wait on the Lord will renew their strength.", "But those who wait on the Lord shall renew their strength. They shall mount up with wings like eagles, they shall run and not be weary, they shall walk and not faint." (Isaiah 40:31 NKJV). This waiting is giving me confidence that I need to soar to a higher level. Biblical teaching has it that God will give you a Word, test you on that Word. You cannot fail the test if you want to go to another level. It is better said that God is bringing you to another level. While we are being tested, we abide under His wings.

One revelation that I have had is that my life has not changed merely by the passage of time. Rather, my life has been changed by decisions, which have changed my conduct, which changed my character, which obviously has changed my destiny. I am more inclined to choose life nowadays.

One of the Seven Principles of the Nguzo Saba, Swahili, is Kuumba (Creativity): to do all that we can in the way that we can in order to leave our community more beautiful and beneficial than we inherited it. This Principle of Kuumba refers to man's Godly purpose. Unfortunately, I have come to observe that man, without consulting his Spiritual Father, acts irrationally many times and does more harm than good in the Earth.

As I build my knowledge base, I have also come to know that the Principle of Kuumba is not restricted to the physical creation, but to the relationships of mankind as well. We are to be peacemakers, restoring good will among our brothers and sisters. We are to do good deeds toward our brethren and empower them to come up to the level where they can contribute to kingdom building.

We know that God is love and that as man has disobeyed many times over the years, God repeatedly extends his mercy toward man and allows him to continue to reside in the place that he was ordered to operate in, this Earth.

There are those who I have restrained displays of affection for because of fear that they would not return the love that I had for them. And as I mature, becoming more Christ-like, I am finding that I do them and myself harm because withholding love causes emotional strain and that emotional strain over time leads to depression. Then that depression can mutate and produce bitterness, which is something that nobody wants to experience. Bitterness is so damaging to the soul of man that man might never overcome the results of bitterness. Bitterness dislodges one's ability to trust.

While I do not wish to cast pearls on swine, I now realize that it is worth the risk of loving those hard to love as sometimes I can win them over to Christ. Winning souls to Christ is one of the most significant things that a believer can do. Of course, I realize that I would have to commit to giving the unbeliever this service because the hard to love person is not readily open to my attempts. I wonder if I have this same effect on others who try to love me, and I reject them.

My conscious tells me that there is a strong connection between love and need. So, I must learn to learn to love in different ways. And sometimes love must be restrained or take on another hue than that of passion, which is red. Sometimes love finds itself needing to have the hue of blue. Sometimes those needing love cannot hear you because 'your love hue' is not lined up with their needs. One can easier share sacrificial love if she is willing to change her hue of love. I have come to know as well, that love is multifaceted, like the colors in a prism. There might be different hues of love intermingled simultaneously.

I have learned that there is a reward for promoting Jesus. One of the ways that we can get the reward is to model walking like Jesus walked on the Earth. We can go about doing good for one another, showing sacrificial love. This sacrificial love, known as Agape Love, elevates one to a higher level than that of physical passion. Agape Love involves physical passion and sacrificial acts to help others. I must believe and trust that Jesus is not going to be nor command that I love unless it is the thing to do. It is the Law. Jesus said, "Love ye one another." John 13:34 NKJV.

Another way that we can model what our purpose is would be to carry out the command of the Resurrected Christ in the Great Commission, (Matthew 28:18-20 KJV), to go into all nations, baptizing them in the name of the Father and of the Son and of the Holy Spirit, teaching them to do all things that He has commanded the believer to do. Believers share their testimony, which can become wings for others to become believers like themselves.

This works because, every living thing reproduces its own kind. For example, sheep reproduces sheep. Believers then reproduce believers. Disciples create disciples. Jesus was talking to the 11 disciples when he mandated the Great Commission.

I think that now the reader and I are on the same page about purpose. Jesus knows our purpose. Everything from Alpha to Omega is about Jesus. When the Universe and everything in it was created, it was about

Jesus. When the Battle of Armageddon is fought, it is about Jesus. He gives me the victory. Therefore, I must pattern my life like unto that of Jesus. I am trying this spiritual journey and I really like its benefits: joy and peace among various others. I do not focus on the natural as much, now that I know that the supernatural is more important. God is not natural. God is Spirit. God is eternal and is my source, which is what I want to have abundant life now and eternal life when I leave this Earth.

I see my life purpose being slow to manifest, like that of Abram. Abram lived at his father's house until he was 75. Abram saw no need to leave his father's house until God called him out and changed his name to Abraham. God changed his name so that He could see himself no longer the codependent Abram, but rather Abraham, who God wanted him to grow into. In Hebrew Names the meaning of the name Abraham is Father of a great multitude. Whereas Abram just means father. There's a big difference between the two names. When God changes your name, I believe that something big is about to happen.

I did not have a life as good as Abram, though. I had to leave my home at the age of 18. I was blessed to have some place to go, or I would have been a casualty. I do not believe that I would have survived. I did not have transportation; no job and I was a young female. I chose to go off to college as I was in a pre-college program already. By the time I went to college, my bread winner had been deceased at least eight years. Had I not gone to college; I would have been homeless then rather than later. I would not have anyone living at home with me. I would have been home alone. At least at college, I could live in the Dormitory and other people would be around. Tougaloo College became home to me for a while.

Reality kicked in on the final day of high school. It had not occurred to me that all my sisters were gone on to pursue their futures in other cities. School was out for the summer, and I would be going to the Summer Program, Upward Bound, which would begin in about a week. But where was Mama? It was getting dark, and she was not home. I went to our substitute mother's house about a half mile away, told her about my problem and was allowed to spend the night. What I refer to as substitute mother was a woman in the community that looked out for us children because my family had supported her over the years. And because my sisters and her children went to school and played together. When Mama had not come home for a couple of days, a search took place to get her to come home. Mama often had unexplained absences from the home. This time, she was possibly out scouting for someplace to live herself as I was going to be gone all summer and then off to college about 90 miles away. Staying home alone was not a problem for me if my sisters were going to be home with me when nightfall came. But now they were not there to protect me. They were all gone to Chicago or to St. Louis to continue their livelihoods.

I felt more alone and frightened than I ever had. I did something that I had never done before when I realized that I was home alone. I cried out to God. I cried as if it was raining. My tears were flooding my face under clear skies. He obviously heard my cry. He gave me the idea to go to the neighbor's home and to not try to stay home alone. There were no longer any tame animals on this barren farm even. Even the one dog that we had was gone. This barrenness was a desolate and lonely feeling penetrating my soul; worse than the way you feel when you are physically lost. I could not see my way. I needed protection. I probably would have been even more afraid had I lived in a city and did not have any friends. I could have gone to my brother's house, but I knew that the niece that I had played with as a child was gone to St. Louis to Job Corps. I also was not thinking clearly. For once, I was at a loss for direction. My brother's house was farther away than our substitute mother's. I went there. The sunset was on the horizon. This was one of the greatest manifestations that I had experienced in my life. I would have to depend on God for guidance and my ability to survive. I did not believe that He would allow me to fail in my effort to survive.

However, at this stage of my life, my believing that all things were possible, I was not wise enough to see that the circumstances and situations happening to me were not by my power, not by my knowledge or by my wisdom. It would be many years for my carnal mind and my spiritual mind to collide and steer me in the right direction.

I never told others in college that I was technically homeless. I had defense mechanisms in place to make me look like someone that I was not. Yes, we had a house. But I was not ready to live alone. On Holidays, I would tag along with other students, who would invite me to go home with them. I learned a great deal from those visits. I saw that those students were poor economically, like me. Yet they were not homeless in that their parents were very much present in the home and that they had parental guidance. It humbled me to know that they liked me so much that they wanted to share their homes with me. The visits were also a good distraction to keep my mind off my problems surrounding my home life. It helped me to learn that the students that I visited were also on a mission to take control of their lives and divorce their parents. I was wishing that I had parents. I did not try to counsel them on their anxiety, as I should have done. However, I was feeling that I would give a million dollars to live in a home where there was love and someone who cared about what I was doing out there in the world. I could act so well that other students would envy me. I acted as if I had it all together. I had stopped crying when my mother left home when I was a toddler. I was now an adult. I had a huge amount of pride. This pride fed my motivation to try to be all that I could be. Afterall, I was a Raglin. I was Buster's kid. I would not let the enemy 'see me sweat'.

I remember going home with one of my Sorority Sisters for the Christmas Break in Hattiesburg, MS when I was in college. I enjoyed the visit very much. Although my Sorority Sister was an upper-class student, I saw that she had a very structured home life. She had a 10 o'clock p. m, curfew. I envied her. Nobody cared what time I went and came home nor who I came and went with. I was just expected to use good judgment and to protect my own skin.

Life and observation of other biblical and life changing legends has taught me that the more difficult and different your journey and the longer it takes you to reach your destiny, the bigger your assignment is to be. I will be transparent here and state that even today, I experience a sense of fear when I ponder what He would have me to do to aid in kingdom building. I now realize that I must trust that He would be doing the work through me and that I am just a vessel. I find myself hanging out at church far more than I did when I was leaning to my own understanding about who and whose I am and how my life should be. I did not see God's Hand orchestrating and guiding my path until much later in life.

I also know that once an organism stops growing, it dies. Realizing that I am not dead, I obviously have not reached my destiny at the ripe old age of 71. To put it another way, I have not accomplished my purpose for being born. And I am aware that I am not to shine when the light is not on me. In other words, I do not have to be aggressive, jealous and envious because my time to shine brighter is currently not apparent. When it is time for me to shine brighter, I will know it. I do know that I am a star and that all stars shine. I do not crave the limelight as some do. When I sing or speak it is either to glorify God or to edify the audience to which I am presenting. However, there are times when I have a difficult time smoldering the urge to compete with other stars when they are shining.

It scares me that my purpose could be one that I do not wish to do because of my insecurities and self-doubt, which I became aware of later in life. However, it gives me a bit of consolation to learn that I am not too much different from many others. God was shaping Moses for his job for over 70 years. Moses, just like myself made excuses and leaned to his own understanding. It is difficult for man to think like God. God would not reveal His plan to Moses too soon because Moses would have become discouraged and messed it up. I cannot help thinking about how Moses did not learn his purpose until he was 80 years old, and man his purpose was big! Moses would deliver millions of people by using his God-given Rod, parting the waters and leading them across the Red Sea on dry land. That was awesome! This act was unimaginable to Moses or to anyone else. God did the assigning and Moses obeyed God. Joshua, Moses' predecessor, would do something remarkably similar when he used Moses' Rod and parted the waters, leading the Israelites across the Jordan River.

And then, Abraham did not produce the seed of the promised son, Isaac until he was one hundred years old. God keeps His promises. God's promises come with Blessings attached. God's promises shall come to pass. Deuteronomy 28. NKJV. I personally believe that promises are often delayed because of the maturity of the person to which the promise was made. This situation also applies to nations. One nation for sure is Israel.

Purpose is not something you sneeze about. If I could claim to be religious here, I would say that if one knows and pursues his purpose, he is being obedient and as a result he receives the Blessing described in the Holy Bible mostly in (Deuteronomy 28:1-14). This Blessing was on the lives of Adam, Abraham, Moses, and other biblical characters who obeyed God. I firmly believe that this Blessing is conditional and requires something of us. If one is disobedient, the opposite side of the Blessing is the Curse. It is obvious that over time, man just has not been able to be obedient to God's Commands and God has continuously been merciful and loving. God has adjusted several times the contracts that He had with man over time, allowing man to continue to live in the Earth.

God commands and makes provision for man to keep those commands. God gives us provision that oftentimes we are not aware of. Moses was questioned by God and prompted to use what he had in his hand. When Moses used his rod, magical things began to happen. We are often not aware of what we have in our hand. We search all over for help, when we already have all the help that we need. God has placed talents and gifts within each of us to equip us to achieve our destiny. There is a secular statement that holds much truth, "The best helping hand that you will find is at the end of your wrist." (Paraphrasing Audrey Hepburn who said that if you need a helping hand, it is at the end of your arm). Audrey Hepburn went on to say that not only do you have a helping hand for yourself, but you also have another to help others. We are co-dependent. And when we blend all our gifts and talents, we can live in harmony.

I have been told that the situation and circumstances surrounding my birth created an arduous story. Most women are not in labor for two to three days before delivery like Mama was with me. Most women can normally deliver a baby with the help of a midwife. Mama had delivered eight with the help of the midwife, but not with me. The midwife gave up and dispatched Daddy to walk a mile to get my brother to come in his truck to take Mama to the hospital to deliver me. That was a one-day ordeal. Mama was forced to ride for almost 100 miles to get to a hospital to give birth in the cold and frigid month of February. When Mama finally got to the hospital, she was forced to convince the medical staffs that she could not deliver me naturally, she had a Caesarian Delivery. This was about two days after getting to the hospital. As the story goes, Mama breast fed eight other children, but not me. I am not certain that the painful birth had anything to do with Mama's decision to leave Daddy before I was three years old. I thank God that she never made me feel guilty for causing her so much pain.

Nobody seemed to consider that Mama could have been a victim of post-partum depression as her mood and her conversation changed and that she had somehow decided to leave the security of Daddy and the four of us there with him.

The mindset of the day was that if a woman was being abused, she should stay and take her punishment and sometimes it meant death. I could see that Daddy was jealous and very controlling, but I only witnessed his physically hitting her once. I am thinking that perhaps a few years later would have been a far more appropriate time for Mama to leave Daddy. Leaving a man at home with four young girls ranging in age from 7 to 3 was not logical and out of season. It was insane. It just seems to me now that she should have left him before having four children by him. It seems to me that she was too smart to be in a toxic relationship for about ten years before making up her mind to leave. Although Mama had three children by Daddy before she married him, it seems to me that she had not thought through her situation before tying the knot with Daddy. When Mama came back home to prevent us from going to foster care after Daddy died, she would tell of how Daddy was so jealous and would tie up his mule and sit outside behind her chimney with his gun across his lap waiting to see if a man was visiting Mama. She shared that Daddy would fall asleep and snore so loudly that he would wake her up and have her thinking that there was some wild animal out there. So, she had to know that he was insanely jealous before she married him. I quired that possibly Mama married Daddy when she did was because she learned that she was pregnant with me. Oh yes, Daddy was building a new house. But was that a good reason?

I remember her saying to Daddy, "Forget about your house, your land and your children. I'm going to have the pleasures of my life." Although I did not know exactly what 'pleasures of one's life' meant at age two, I soon learned what it meant by the stark reality that she had left home. Reality soon kicked in and I did not have a Mama.

I awakened one morning while sitting in bed, I looked out across the fields and saw what I related to as Santa Claus going over a fence with a big brown bag on his back. I was later to learn that this Santa Claus was Mama with her clothes in a Croker Sack. Daddy being the great hunter that he was had trailed her and spotted the clothes because she had become entangled in the barbed wire fence separating the bordering property from Daddy's. Daddy brought the clothes home and Mama had gotten away. I do not remember how he told my older sisters when they came home from school. I just had an eerie feeling that Mama had left us. The next day, I was very lonely because my playmate, Mama was not there. I experienced my first episode of loneliness and darkness, which I later learned was depression in my life at two and a half years old. I was traumatized. My trust was broken. I feared what would happen had Daddy decided to leave me alone as well. I was devastated.

This insanity of Mama leaving Daddy caused turmoil throughout the community. Everybody was thinking that Mama had wealth and every-thing that others wanted and needed. Well, wealth was not everything Mama wanted and needed. Yet, we children did not suffer from much other than our countenances, perhaps. Daddy provided well. Neither did he talk negatively to me about Mama. Actually, Daddy's silence painted the picture to me that I was free to see that she was just a woman who was self-centered and needed to grow up. This was my thinking at such an early age. Mama had taught me well during the short time that she was with me. Before Mama left, I was independent. I learned to cook many things by observing her cook. I just could not get the gist of those buttermilk biscuits that she made from scratch every morning. I also learned some things not to do in the kitchen. I witnessed the pressure cooker top flying up to the ceiling on a couple of occasions. When I saw her jump back, I knew that this was not something that I wanted to do. I made a mental note that I would hot comb my own hair one day because she would not do it. She hot combed my sister's hair though. I 'manned up' and became the old soul that I was by the time I started going to school. Mama also helped me to see that Jesus loved me. She would sing Zion Songs as she worked around the house. Mama never worked the fields. She did not have to leave the house for anything during the day. Mama just told Daddy what she wanted to cook from his huge vegetable garden and Daddy brought it to her. The garden entrance was boxed in between the house and the barn. Mama was always in the kitchen. She cooked two major meals daily. I never once heard Daddy complain about her cooking. Before they married, Mama worked in the kitchen of the white family who her parents sharecropped with. However, if she was to be married to Daddy, she could no longer work in a white man's kitchen.

Before I started going to school, I taught Daddy that he was not a good babysitter. Daddy had gotten up early one morning intending to work in his fields and rush back home to cook my breakfast. This was my opportunity to hot comb my hair, I thought. He had left me a nice fire in the fireplace. The coals were very red. I went to the kitchen, got a fork and put it in the fireplace. This would straighten my hair as it looked a lot like the pressing comb that mama used to straighten my sisters' hair. This incident burned my hair and the curtains, which I grabbed to put the flame out in my hair. This started a flame running up the curtains, which I was lucky to snatch down and throw them in the fireplace. When Daddy came home, he knew something was wrong. The stench from the burning curtains and hair was very strong.

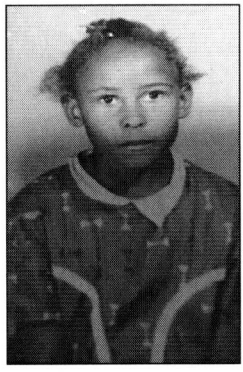

I am in the Third Grade on this picture. My hair had grown back in the top. The photo was taken after recess. My oldest sister of the four of us had styled my hair. I became disheveled during recess. I played hard by myself.

It was depressing and lonely to look around and see that all the other children in school and the neighboring children in the community had mothers and I did not have one. It was also depressing to see people in the community look at us with sympathy. I would want to say something negative and lash out at them. Somehow, I kept my feelings to myself. As I grew older, I learned that Mama did not raise any of her nine children. I heard my mother's father say that he had spoiled Mama. He called her "Froggy". I was a grownup then and Granddaddy was almost 100 years old when he told me that Mama was spoiled. Although I had not questioned him further about how she was spoiled by him, I guessed that he meant that he never disciplined her and made her accountable for her moral conduct. He and Grandma would end up helping her raise five of her other children. Daddy was not having that. Although he did not marry Mama before they had me, he would support his other children that he had by her along with the other two that she had at home by other men. Those relationships had not worked out for her either.

As I grew older and studied social work, I learned that the average number of times the abused female leaves a toxic domestic relationship is an average of 10, if she is not murdered beforehand. Mama just stayed and endured the pain. Mama had prior relationships and a marriage where the husband was and reportedly an abuser. She knew that Daddy was jealous years before I was born.

Leading up to her departure, I had only witnessed Daddy physically abusing her once when we were walking from church one night through the woods. It was extremely dark as there was no moon out. Although I could not see him slap her on the butt with a sugar cane knife that he had left somewhere outside the church when he came to walk us home. I did not see a knife when he came into the church. I got the knowledge that Daddy was hiding the weapon from the community busybody, who just happened to be a man. This man would snoop around and see what others were up to. He had nothing else to do with his time. Nevertheless, the fact that I was unaware of any abuse, does not mean that there were not times when I was out of ear and eyeshot.

Mama always called Daddy, 'Mister Buster'. That was not very romantic. Afterall, she was twenty years younger than he. Some of his first set of children were older than she. So many of my nieces and nephews are older than me. And many are now deceased.

Although people in the community looked upon us girls with pity when we went out sometimes, because we did not have a mother. We soon learned to dress up and become fashionistas. The gossip about the separation spread all the way to the school that we attended in Camden, MS. I did not realize until lately that Camden is a very large rural community, and our farm was bordering Camden, MS. on the East, which is in Madison County and Holmes County on the North. We attended Couparle Church and school in Camden. We got our mail from Goodman, MS, which is Holmes County. We would walk almost two miles to get our mail from Route 2, Box 34, Goodman, MS. Luckily, people were honest back then and would not ambush each other's mail. Mama would order clothes from fashion magazines, and they would come to the mailbox.

The Church and the school were ten to fifteen miles apart. The schoolteachers were caring and genuinely concerned about the child's education. This was a big help. I aspired to be 'Teacher's Pet'. I got all 'A's'. The compensation paid off. I did not realize that I was compensating. Those who could not compete with my grades, disliked me. It was a friendly competition. Those who saw the genius in me, aspired to be me. Back then, a student did not hate to the point of murder as we hear of nowadays.

I now realize that I was a late bloomer. I did not experience some things that my older siblings and associates experienced at ages much younger than I. And, when I finally experienced them, I had an 'aha' moment. I do now wonder though if I were just not paying attention and learning from the experiences of my older siblings and their playmates because I would rather not get the many whippings they would get from Mama. So, I isolated myself, becoming deeply involved in exploring the vast world around me. I had over 100 acres (about half the total floor space of the Pentagon) of land to roam around on. Oftentimes I would trespass onto the friendly neighbors' properties as well as on the 50 acres (about twice the area of Chicago's Millennium Park) of my Daddy.

I had learned in school to always be on good behavior so that the parents of my friends would take a liking to me. I was often invited to have sleep overs with my friends. Those students, who befriended me would sell me to their parents as a high caliber student, just as I was. I had a good reputation as an honor student, who later became, "Miss Jackson High and co-valedictorian of my senior class. I now can chalk it up to say that in many ways, "I was not a late bloomer". I developed physically on target. I just did not have the same interests as my older sisters and their friends. I viewed life from another paradigm. Marriage was not in my interest as I had lost my first love.

My schoolteachers saw something in me and took a liking to me. One of them saw that I had talent to sing and perform dramatically. I was then off to attend talent shows and to compete against other students statewide. I was very confident, a rising star. And then I experienced a traumatic molestation.

The molestation happened as the result of my wandering alone at age 10. I noticed that the experience was inappropriate. There was a spiritual change in my psyche. I was a virgin, and the experience was not pleasurable. It hurt. I would soon get my period, which was to take place in the classroom when I was fourth grade. My classmate, a male student sitting next to me saw the blood on my finger as I had touched the blood running down my leg. He thought that I had cut my finger. I got myself to the restroom, a 'toilet' behind the school building, used a lot of toilet paper to clean myself up with and padded my panties. This got me through the day. I had already been schooled by my older sisters that this day was coming and that I would have to learn feminine hygiene. The Health Class in school also addressed the subject of menstruation. I do not recall birth control being a part of the Health Class, though. I really needed this subject to be addressed because shortly after I was molested, I got my period. I rationalized, 'those grownups were having sex, so it was okay to do it if children kept it a secret. And it was not so physically painful the next time with the perpetrator. This time, I did not fight him off, allowing him to molest me from time to time. I knew it was wrong and that he had a girlfriend. Somehow, I still liked the attention from the other sex. I cooperated without a fight as it was not going to take a long time as we were standing up and would have to go someplace shortly thereafter. Probably what saved me from an early pregnancy was that the perpetrator was soon married and moved to another city far away from me.

The molestation and the body changes had an awkward and devastating effect on my psyche. I did not have the self-confidence that I had before having sex. If this is what is called a broken spirit, I had one. I would have flash backs and my emotions would become unbalanced and unstable. I would have flashbacks when I was performing on talent shows and 'oratorical' contests. I would freeze in the middle of a speech not realizing what the trigger was. Once I was performing and forgot that we had a costume change in my miscellaneous act the night before the contest when I was at the home of the teacher. I recall that the talent show was on a Saturday, which meant that I would have to spend the night with the teacher. I was already beginning to feel awkward around my superiors for reasons that I could not decipher. I experienced what it is like to have low self-esteem. The teacher changed the costume so that I could save time changing between acts while singing my songs. She did not realize that I had practiced so much the other way that I was on auto pilot. I simply pulled off the top of my costume and just had a bra on top. I must admit that what I was cited for was hardly worth getting a citation for in today's world. I came in second place. My citation was for poor showmanship. I felt very badly as I had disappointed my teacher. I don't think I ever forgave myself for that incident. I just had to keep going. I was not reprimanded for making the glitch.

After losing the District Contest, I would not be going to the State Competition. I was upset. I was not to go home with the female teacher after the contest. She sent me home with a male teacher. Before we got to my home, the teacher pulled over and propositioned me for sex. I was flabbergasted! This was unimaginable! I did not see him as someone I would be interested in having sex with. I had a deep respect for him and having sex with him would seem like having sex with my father. Thank God, he did not force me. I could only assume that he was doing this because his wife was pregnant. Or did everyone know now that I was sexually active outside of marriage.

When I was first molested, Daddy was alive. I cannot remember what my rationalization was that I did not tell him. We were close enough that I could tell him. I can only imagine that Daddy would have gotten his shot gun and exterminated the rapist from the planet. I was disappointed that I was molested, but I have yet to understand when the devastation took place in my soul. It is crazy! A bitterness took over me. Loss of virginity at the wrong time and with the wrong person is a devastating situation to a girl and probably to a boy as well.

On another occasion, I was in an 'oratorical' contest. We had to make our speeches without referring to notes. I was almost at the end of my speech, had a flashback and froze. I lost the contest. I had a deficit in my confidence, and I did not know why at that time. Even today, I have difficulty understanding, even now how I allowed the molestation to damage me psychologically. I much later in life came to know that the after effect of molestation carries symptoms of Post-Traumatic Stress Syndrome and occasionally a feeling of helplessness. Agoraphobia, strongholds of love-hate relationship, and even a pattern of being molested by other males and not prosecuting them are also symptoms. Another symptom of molestation grief entails letting the perpetrator off the hook, self-blaming and rationalization that the victim deserved the molestation. Low self-esteem kicks in big time. When the perpetrator is a superior, the victim fears the loss of affection from the perpetrator in the future. While none of these symptoms hold truth, they are very real to the victim. Undoubtedly the perpetrator will become uneasy when he encounters the victim in everyday settings. He will pretend not to know the victim or act as if nothing happened. However, the act of molestation carries with it mental and spiritual effects that penetrates the soul.

After research, I learned that there is a difference between molestation and rape. The difference is not based on the degree of violence, it is based on the age of the victim. Otherwise, the two terms would be synonymous? Both are damaging to the psyche and the soul of the victim. The only difference tends to be inserted for legal reasons. The victim's age up to fourteen decides that the victim is molested. Otherwise, the victim is raped from fifteen and up.

To the victim of a former molestation, there is the fear of saying "No" in the future because of the above-mentioned symptoms. The fear is embedded within as if it is a demonic spirit. But until the victim stands up and adamantly says "No," the cycle continues, and the victim falls farther and farther down the spectrum of low self-esteem.

As the result of molestation, I am often hypervigilant about situations I get myself into with the other sex. Being in isolated environments with certain people makes me feel very uneasy. I have a sense of which males I can risk being alone with. I am not saying that this always realistic, but it is a delusion that I have. However, this is a defense mechanism that I have regarding keeping myself safe. And often I sabotage myself from taking advantage of opportunities that could be valuable to me because of this fear of being raped at the ripe old age that I am now. One example of my triggers against rape is to never be the first attendee at an event or place. Nor can I be the last to leave. This fear is remarkably like that I have when I walk upon a dead body as I have done this more than once before.

I was nudged into liking boys and took my lead from my sisters. Liking boys was the one area that I felt inclined to copy from my older sisters. It was pleasant to entertain boys, and Mama was gone and could not punish me if whatever we were doing warranted punishment.

"The mind is a doorway to the heart. (Whatever you think about goes to the heart and you will end up doing it unless you repent"). Do I really understand what this quote is saying? This is one manifestation that I experienced and learned at the ripe old age of 38. I must not have been paying attention to the teacher when she taught me that. I still struggle with this area of my life. I do a lot of rationalizing.

Dr. Dale Bronner, Pastor of Word of Lifes Ministries taught me that if you think about or better stated that if you meditate on something that is immoral or unethical for a long/extended period, you will end up doing that you are thinking about. And when you do what you were thinking about and it is morally wrong, you must repent. Repent is a Hebrew way of saying, "Stop doing what you are doing." "Stop doing the thing that is immoral or unethical immediately." Of course, some are unable to repent, per Bishop Steven G. Thompson, My Pastor, because "They never did anything". Let that marinate.

I was confident that Daddy would not punish us for liking boys because he had not displayed any serious dislike for boys other than the one time when my sister next to the oldest received a letter from a boy when she was in the eighth or ninth grade. Daddy found the letter and scolded her for getting involved with boys at her early age. Of course, she did not stop liking boys. She liked them even more. She just got smarter, hid the letter out of Daddy's sight the next time and referred to it from time to time. She would dance and prance as she read it over and over. She would read the letter over and over, "Roses are red. Violets are blue. The angels in heaven know that I love you." She was entertaining to watch. Soon thereafter, this boy went back to Iowa from whence he came, and she was on to another admirer.

Daddy's raging at my sister about the letter from the boy, did not deter her from seeing boys. I would be matched up with the younger brother of my sister's boyfriends, just to keep them entertained while she would seriously court and get intimate with the older brother. I took notes, believing that what I was being taught was the thing to do. I learned to take control of my relationships. Afterall, I was a fighter and a survivor.

Daddy rarely used corporal punishment. He would rant and rave, but rarely took off his belt and gave us a lashing as long as Mama was home. Mama was left with the chore of punishing us girls. Mama did not spare using the switch, usually from the peach tree.

Corporal punishment is the least effective method for correcting negative behavior. It is just a bandage, primarily good for a temporary period. If the parent is not willing to check to ensure that the act is not repeated, they are certain to see repeat offender relapse. I got whippings from Mama with the peach tree switch, daily for begging for biscuits around Noontime than any other negative behavior at my tender age of two. I would forget about the whipping I got the day before at the same time, even though Mama would make me get the switch from the peach tree. And all I can remember about the punishment today is that I would be swinging in the air wailing profusely as she was whipping me. I do not recall any pain. I did not understand that dinner was for the field hands and that I needed to wait for them to come to the house to eat before I got the biscuit. Daddy would intervene and yell at her, "Put my baby down." Little did he know that those words would be coming reality in a few days. I would become just his baby because Mama left him as she promised that she would.

This is evidence that children are resilient. I grieved for a brief spell after Mama left, and then I learned to adjust to not having a mother. My sisters helped me a lot by not openly grieving. They also pitched in and nurtured me. They did such an excellent job, that I accepted the fact that I had no mother. I was resilient. I at once became independent. I never felt that I could not survive. I also was left to Daddy to babysit me when the other children went off to school daily. Daddy never made me feel that I was a nuisance. I had no idea that he could not babysit me and work in his fields, some of which were about a quarter of a mile away from the house.

Daddy's land was remote and there was no major thoroughfare separating the neighboring properties. Boundaries were set up with barbed wire fences and signs of "Posted, Stay Out." Most of the fences needed repair as they did not deter anyone from encroaching on them. They were barbed wire fences and most of the strands were rusted and broken. It was just understood that one did not enter the property and begin squatting, despite the landowner's absence for years. Daddy was the only subsistence farmer around besides his son, who lived at least a mile and a half away. He had livestock and was forced to keep his fences intact. The barbed wire fences were the only boundaries separating the properties. Daddy would walk his property often because he needed to ensure that there was no invasion from hostile neighbors.

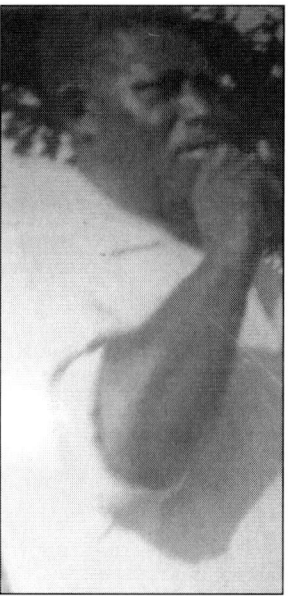

Daddy in 1952 after church

Oftentimes my vast imagination and curiosity would have me venturing a long way from home. This was a habit of mine for as long as I can remember. What puzzles me today is that nobody came looking for me. What I was doing was extremely dangerous as I would be out of range of my family, who would not have heard me had I screamed for help. I was a loner, and it took many years for me to learn to be careful of going too far astray. I suppose Mama was so busy that she did not realize that I had wandered away from home. Or she thought that I would soon come back home when I got hungry. Mama knew that I played under the house with the chickens and the dogs oftentimes. The clay dirt underneath the house was clean and not dusty. I learned to navigate the 'compost' from the chickens, the cats and the dogs that found sanctuary under there when she had visitors that I was not familiar with.

I usually wandered in the mornings while Mama was cooking biscuits. She knew that I loved her homemade biscuits. I can only guess that she just knew I would show up when the biscuits were done cooking.

I remember wandering away from home with no clothes on or, I would have on a dress and no panties. Sometimes I would be caught wandering half naked by my grownup neighbor, who would turn me 'Sunnyside Up', give me a big spank and tell me not to let her catch me away from home again with no panties on. She would then carry me back to Mama and report me. I felt guilty then, but soon forgot. I was a repeat offender, relapsing many times until one day it was entrenched in me that I needed to wear panties because all the other girls wore panties. I did not want to be so different after I was shamed by my neighbor. The turn sunny side up worked.

I still wonder why nobody came looking for me when I wandered at such an early age. I have never seen the need to have so many others around me. As I author this book, I am watching a show where a two-year-old wandered or was kidnapped. While I have deep sympathy for the family of the lost child, I also wonder why nobody sent crowds of search parties out to find me. This reminds me of the movie where the mother felt that two dogs were too much for the family to handle when a stray dog happened to join the family. Then one day the toddler wandered into the woods. A search party was sent out into the woods to look for the child. When the toddler was found by the grandfather with the stray dog that the mother was planning to get rid of, the mother had a swift change of heart. Now, she was glad to have the stray. I cried tears of joy when the boy and the stray dog were found in the woods by the grandfather. I was thinking about how I wish that someone would have declared me lost sometimes and came looking for me. Or at least warn me of the dangers lurking out there. There were crop duster airplanes. I would fall face down in the dirt until the plane flew over. I was later to learn that there were also monstrous snakes roaming the properties as well. There was enough foliage and forest for Big Foot to be out there as well. Of course, I did not know about the snakes and Big Foot at that time. The snakes would show up much later.

Racism

When I was growing up in Mississippi, racism nor Jim Crow Law phased me. The way I was raised, there was no need for me to interact with those of the other race, Caucasian. I only interacted with was void of such stuff. either. Obviously, I was ignorant to the situations because I was sheltered from them unknowingly. Mama was a stay-at-home mother. Daddy shopped for food staples in bulk, once or twice a year.

We went to church occasionally as a family before Mama left home. We did not go to church every Sunday because Daddy would have to hitch his two mules to the Wagon, sit in the Wagon about thirty minutes waiting for Mama to get dressed, get on the Wagon bed, sit in her straight-back chair that was certain to fall over backwards when Daddy struck the mules in anger for takeoff. Mama had to look good. She would sit in the chair powdering her face and putting on lipstick when Daddy struck the mules to jerk off with a fast pace. My sisters would have to set Mama's chair with her seated in it back upright while the wagon was rolling. She was not a tiny woman. We were always late getting to the church, Couparle A.M.E. where we had membership. Our church was at least five miles away. Other times, we would walk to my older sister's church, Mount Mary Baptist Church, about a mile and a half away or another church, True Light Apostolic Church about two miles away from our home. We called True Light the 'sanctified' church. We went there because one of my sisters was becoming engaged to a member there. I liked it there because they were so lively. I thought their code of dress for women was a bit overdone and awkward, but otherwise I was onboard with the joyful noise as they praised God with tambourines and a single guitar played by the Pastor. The 'Apostolic Church' is much the same in all ways today, except the women are no longer arrayed in white robes. There was very little music played at Couparle and Mount Mary churches. Couparle had a piano that was seldom played. But the deacons led a spiritual and uplifting service. The Watt's Hymns were prominent for Devotion. A deacon would kneel and pray for a long time.

All the congregations we attended were one hundred percent black. The white people attended Shrock and Shiloh Churches. Black people were not allowed to attend those churches and Black people did not seem to want to attend them anyway. I never saw any Caucasian people at Black Churches either. It was not a big deal that everyone at church was black like me. My sisters and I went to a segregated school. We felt that it was normal to do so. Segregation of African American children and Caucasian children allowed for inequality in how finance for education between the two different races, the colored and the whites was distributed. Ms. Velma Ware Jackson obviously knew and was given privy to how the economics of education was distributed and she fought to have a brick-and-mortar school built from the ground up. This was justice. This new school building was an icon of what was soon to take place in the State of Mississippi. "No justice, no peace. No peace, no justice." This was the cry of the people there in Camden, Mississippi around the time that I was going into Middle School.

And we were excited when the new school was built, not knowing at the time that the black superintendent, Ms. Velma Ware Jackson had such struggle with Jim Crow Law and Racism to get the school built. The former school, Camden Elementary and Camden High School consisted of a Church, and three frame buildings.

We did not think much about the White (Caucasian) children being bused off to some other school. We did not socialize with White People. As I grew older, I began to wonder a little bit about comments that were made indirectly to me and around me about racism. Somehow, they would do what people call, 'went over my head.' Older people did not talk openly about religion, racism, slavery, and sex. And children were spared the burden of knowing too much unnecessary stuff. It seemed that the only thing my parents wanted was for the children to go to school. And they did not even talk about why it was so important to get good education. I was just impressed that they put a great deal of emphasis on getting the kids off to school. I was not able to go to school right away. But I was curious about the hype and could not wait until I was of age to go to school to learn. Although I did not like strangers, I had no problem with being in the presence of kids my age.

Sunday afternoon was the day for visits from boys. I recall that one Sunday, one of my sister's boyfriend came to visit and brought along his younger brother. My older sisters would set the stage for the visit. They would ensure that everyone had a place to sit. They would set two chairs in the living room so that my sister's boyfriend's brother would sit in one chair and the vacant chair was for me to sit and entertain him while my sister and her boyfriend would find someplace out of sight of my daddy, who would be in the adjacent room. I was disturbed by one of the boys, because he did not have a conversation and he was very timid. He would just sit and wait for his brother to get ready to leave. I would try to start up a conversation with him and would get nowhere. He gave all closed ended answers to my open questions. And I would become flustered when he did not try to talk to me. I found out later that my other sister was liking him. She accused me of taking all her boyfriends.

One Sunday, while sitting there trying to entertain the boy who had limited conversation, I looked out across the fields and saw another boy coming to see me. I did not wait for him to get to the house, which was at least a fourth of a mile from the main road. He was walking. I eased out of my chair, left the room, jumped out of the dining room window, and ran away to hide down by the pond. I did not have the courage then and not even today to be confronted by two lovers simultaneously. I had learned from my sister that if there was more than one admirer, the girl needed to keep them apart. I held to this belief and learned that it kept me out of hot water. It seemed like hours before my sister came and found me by the pond. She told me, "You can come to the house, now. They're gone." It took a little convincing for her to get me to come back to the house. I was not going to be in the middle of a fight, not that one would take place. Both guys were on their best behaviors. I knew that Daddy would not tolerate any commotion. He made it plain that he was the 'Captain of the ship'. He sat there in the next room, occasionally clearing his throat. If it were getting late in the evening and the boys had not left by 8 pm, Daddy would start winding his Big Ben Alarm Clock. The boys would get the message that it was their signal to leave, and they would do just that after saying their goodbyes.

A similar incident like this happened to me again when I was in college, but I was again able to circumvent the event by hiding in the dormitory so that neither of the boys could find me.

I was not truly as smart as others had told me that I was. But then, I possibly was smart in comparison to the level of intellect that those praising me had. I was not aware that the depth of my knowledge depended on the intensity of my desire to understand relationship, which would usher me into fellowship. Neither did I know that understanding relationship would determine the timing of my ability to shine. I see now that I had not learned to depend on God because at that time, I did not realize that all I had to do was to trust in the Lord with all my heart and not depend on my own distorted understanding. I did not grow up with Bible Study, nor did I know of the many treasures the Word of God holds. I had no hunger for the Word of God, despite the occasional attendance to Sunday School and devotions that Daddy had with the family.

I was much later to realize that there are many different reasons that others say flattering things to you. I began to question as I became a teenager if I really was as smart as others told me that I was. Maybe they were talking about in books as my knowledge about the importance of having good relationships more so than a head full of knowledge and lacking the wisdom to properly apply this knowledge was deficient. When I reflect on opportunities that I missed in life because of this lack of wisdom, I still feel depressed.

Several opportunities came to mind that I failed to act on. I truly felt that had I acted on them, I would have had a dramatically different outcome in my life. However, I do wonder if I would have been happier had I taken those opportunities.

One of those opportunities was to leave Tougaloo College and attend Tennessee State University after finally being accepted there after I was enrolled in Tougaloo College. I think that one of the reasons that I did not take this opportunity was because one of my teachers had tried to talk me out of attending Tennessee State University. I did not like his reason that I would be pregnant before I was there two weeks. This is not very encouraging, I thought. However, Tougaloo College provided the financial support that I needed to attend the school and Tennessee State University was late into the first semester accepting me.

Another missed opportunity was to drop out of Tougaloo College and go to work for Transworld Airlines at the end of my sophomore year. So glad that I did not do this.

The Airline was bankrupt a few years later and I would not have had a degree of any kind.

I did leave Tougaloo College at the end of my sophomore year and took the opportunity to become an exchange student at Dartmouth College, an All-male Ivy League school in Hanover, New Hampshire. This opportunity was one that I blindly accepted. I was unable to see that I had more unanswered questions than I was able to discern. I was not able to see that I needed counseling far more than just having the knowledge that going there would be free. Going to Dartmouth came with a large sacrifice. There was culture shock. I lived in a warm climate. The onset of winter came shortly after I landed on campus. The early 1970's was a time when there were no portable telephones nor telephones of any kind convenient on campus. Nobody checked on the four of us black females from Tougaloo College for the year that we were gone. Once I was there at Dartmouth College, I was able to get along with some of the students, mostly black. I did not have a roommate. I was not bothered by this. I was dating an upper-class student, who was a Rhodes Scholar. I did not know that a Rhodes Scholarship entailed either. He told me that he would be going to Oxford England and that I should come along with him. I was already traumatized about living in this unfamiliar culture and territory. I had decided that I had taken enough risks already going to Dartmouth College. My friend did not mention how I would be taken care of financially. It probably was to my advantage not knowing that he would be able to house me while he was in school there. I probably would have accepted the offer not having my degree. I liked him a lot. He just did not do a lot of talking about things that mattered. And I was just feeling my way. It was as if I was in the dark and that there was no lighthouse to guide me to the shore. I graciously declined his offer, decided that this was a temporary relationship and resigned my thoughts to going to Tougaloo and completing my senior year. I continue to question my logic about declining this opportunity because when I arrived back at Tougaloo College, I learned that I was homeless, that the relationship that I had with the male student there had dissolved, and I was devastated about the entire situation. Yet, I had a dogged determination to go ahead and get my degree. When I got my degree, not only had I gotten book knowledge, but I had also gone to the 'school of hard knocks'. I learned that there are people who I thought would be willing to help me in a time of crisis, were not. I was surviving day by day. I did not have Daddy to fall back on.

When I was with Daddy, nobody dared disrespect me. 'Buster Raglin' had a reputation of being a warrior. People said that he was mean. I still feel today that I must defend his name even when relatives talk about him and call him mean. He was always nice to me. Others say otherwise, even today. They are referring to things that their older generation had passed down.

I was privy to hear some of Daddy's hilarious war stories. I gleaned from those stories that Daddy had guts and a lot of courage. I oftentimes reflect on the stories when I get in a jam and ask myself, "What would Daddy do?" Sometimes, I assessed that Daddy did not do the right thing. He just happened to be able to live because of his reputation of being resourceful and the grace of God. Today, he probably would have lost his life at the hands of someone who had displaced anger and fear of him.

Courage is displayed when you do something even in the presence of fear. I could see that Daddy was very courageous. I remember Daddy telling me that there were only, two men in the world that he was afraid of. One of them was a man who had a prison record for murdering his wife and the other was the brother of his second wife, who he had divorced. I saw Daddy being brave enough to go to the home of a woman that he thought that he wanted to marry to scare off the man who had murdered his wife. Just short of a duel, the two men were working toward having a standoff. Daddy went to the woman's house one Sunday evening to wait for the man to visit the woman. I was eight or nine years old, standing in the back yard when this very nicely dressed man on a grey Clydesdale horse rode across Daddy's backyard. He was so close to me when I noticed him, I could not run and hide. He tipped his hat at me and kept going in the direction of the woman's house, at least a mile away. I knew who the man was because Daddy had already told us what his plans were that afternoon. I wondered who would win the woman's heart because Daddy did not own a suit and this man was dressed immaculately in a black suit and tie, a black derby hat and well-shined Stetson shoes. Daddy had left home before I saw him, but most likely, he was wearing 'khakis' and a short-sleeved white shirt. Daddy did not spend money on clothes for himself. Luckily Daddy returned home safely.

Daddy liked to tell me jokes and things to make me laugh and think. Daddy was a blacksmith during the Springtime just before the farmers were to break the soil and do the planting of their crops. He would sharpen the plow blades and put shoes on horses. Daddy said that there was a plow point called a 'bulls' tongue'. Daddy said that a black man who was mentally handicapped was told by the white man that he worked for to come to Daddy's shop and get his bull's tongue. Daddy said that he looked across the fields and saw the handicapped man wrestling with one of his bulls. Daddy said that the man also had a knife is his hand and was trying to pry the bull's mouth open. The man was overpowering the bull and was almost successful. Daddy said that he yelled out to the man asking what was doing with his bull. The man yelled back, "Mr. Joe told me to get his tongue." Daddy said that he had a hard time convincing the man that Mr.

Joe was talking about a plow point and that the man needed to let the bull go. I screamed with laughter at this supposedly true story. I still laugh when I think of it.

I was so excited about going to school for the first time that I impressed the teacher with my enthusiasm and my vivid imagination. I wanted to obey and please my teacher. She was extremely nice. My first-grade teacher verbally shared with me that I had a vivid imagination. And I kept my enthusiasm and imagined that I would achieve grandiose things throughout High School.

I missed my mother, but school served as a buffer between my loneliness and heartbreak. The word quickly got around in the community when my mother left home. She grew up in the Camden Community and I later came to know that most of the people living there were kin to her. I recall being comforted by one of the older students in my class who happened to know that I was motherless. The older student was at least 15 years old in the second grade. It was common for students to be behind their proper grade levels because they had to miss so many days from school to harvest their families' crops. The fifteen-year-old female student would pull me down underneath the desks and put her breast in my mouth and tell me to suck it. I did not want to do it. But she would bully me into sucking her breast. Little did she know that I was the only child out of nine that Mama did not breastfeed. I did not understand how she could bully me, and the teacher was there in the classroom. The fifteen-year-old was also bullying other students, especially boys. I am not sure what happened that this student soon stopped coming to school. I could only imagine that she was a dropout because of her promiscuity.

As if the older student's bullying was not enough, my estranged Mama would come to the school unannounced and slide a dress on top of the dress that I was wearing, tie the sash too tightly and run and get in the car with someone she was riding with, drive off and I would not see her again. Obviously, Mama would have attended a funeral at the church across the road from our school.

When I started school, my class was at the church that Mama had attended from her childhood. Murphy Chapel in Camden, Mississippi. This was Mama's family's place of worship. Couparle AME Church also in Camden, Mississippi was Daddy's family's place of worship. Camden is a community expanding for many miles. The town of Camden had about two general stores operating during my school days. There was not a large amount of shopping one could do there. All shopping for clothing and the Madison County Seat was in Canton, Mississippi, twenty miles away.

Times have certainly changed. I am referring to the way school was then and how it is now. I loved my teachers and trusted them. It did not matter that sometimes things would take place where the students were at risk of being harmed. I felt secure at school. In today's world, parents must worry about their children's safety on a continuous basis.

As I mentioned earlier that at that time, it was not uncommon for students to be aged out of the class that they were attending. I studied Mississippi History in the 6th grade. I recall our having a student in his late teens in our class, who could not read. He appeared to be thirty years old. He became laughingstock when the teacher asked him to read. The student called the word but, it. The teacher, short in stature, with the character of an army sergeant, put her hand on her hip, stamped her foot, and said, "Repeat after me, that word is but, Eugene Rice." The student stupidly said verbatim, "That word is but, Eugene Rice." By then, we students were screaming with laughter. We were very cruel. We felt that the student was not entitled to be in our class because he was so much older than us and that he never came to school over five days out of the year. He would come to school, register for the year, and would rarely come back after it was cotton picking time.

Speaking more about safety, I recall that each year around May, a mentally insane woman would come on campus and scare all the teachers and the principals. She would take over the school. She was said to be coming from the State Mental Hospital in Whitfield, Mississippi. I recall there being three different buildings and that she would spend the day visiting each. On one occasion, I recall her coming to my classroom. Our teacher ran out of the room and hid in a closet. I heard later that all of the other teachers ran and left their students to fend for themselves, too. We students were left at the mercy of the insane woman. She gave my class Jitney Jungle Christmas Sales Catalogs and she demanded that we sing 'Rudolph the Red Nosed Reindeer' as she banged on the piano, acting as if she was reading music from her Jitney Jungle book, all out of tune. When she tired of playing with us, she ran outside and started swinging around the flagpole. Sometimes the Principal would have to get his rifle and threaten her. This was the only act that would force her to leave the campus. This patient of Whitfield Asylum, many miles away from Camden Elementary School did not need to be in public without supervision. She obviously was not taking her medications. And her family certainly were not supervising her visits to the home.

It was a good thing that none of the students were physically harmed. We were just terrified. I do not remember my sisters and I telling Daddy about the insane woman's visits. She would only visit one day of the year. I now suspect that she was once a teacher before her breakdown. The insane woman did not prevent us from going to school the next day.

I excelled in school, despite the odds stacked against me. It seems that if someone does not point out to you that something is not right, sometimes you do not see inequality. This takes me back to when slavery was ended and the slaves in Texas were months later finding out that slaves were freed in all other states. The slaves were freed in April and the slaves in Texas did not know until June two years later.

I was co-valedictorian, an unusual designation for high schools to do. The administration had a hard time breaking the tie. Somebody was fighting for me as I was valedictorian alongside my fellow cohort. I thought that there was a fight because the other student was great in subjects of science and mathematics and I was great in English, language, literature and I had an outgoing personality. He was very focused and what we students thought to be inflexible.

Life is Filled
with Swift Transitions

When I became about three years old, I experienced the trauma of parental separation. Only this time, it was my Mama who left Daddy rather than the norm, Daddy leaving Mama. Black men were usually the ones to leave the family with the woman raising the children, I thought. I was forced to adjust to not having a mother quickly enough. Although I was shooting from the hip most of the time, I had to go for what I knew. In the process, I saw that I knew a lot more than I thought I did. I quickly became a little woman, always expected to do the right thing and to take the lead.

Racism was not a real issue for me so far. I was moving along in life with not a large amount of turmoil and very little money, which did not seem to bother me. Miraculously, everything I needed was provided. I took this divine provision for granted. Obviously, it worked because I worked it, I thought. I kept my grades and attendance in school up. I had a real passion and determination to do well in school. I went about my daily activities with diligence. My teachers and my family fed the spirit in me to excel. Being an honor student, high school queen and secretary felt good. I did not focus on what I did not have. I focused on what I had, which was sheer opportunity, and I had the wisdom to take advantage of the opportunity to excel. I started a program called Upward Bound the Summer of my eleventh-grade year in high school. I continued through my senior year and the summer after. I attended the program the summer after I graduated and stayed on campus for my first year in college. I had not heard of the glass ceiling. This was to come later in life, probably when I went to college away from home. I had just formed a level of discipline. I was aiming highly. It mattered to me what others believed about me.

I was surviving. Afterall, all my siblings had left home. Then, when I was in high school before I went away to college, several other traumatic events took place to alter my life. I was becoming depressed about them. The War in Vietnam took place. Many of the young men in my class were drafted, along with my boyfriend, who I thought I would be marrying.

I learned that there was a movement against racism and discrimination and that Dr. Martin Luther King, Jr. Was spearheading this event. I came to know that the entire black community was involved in the movement and that some were jailed in Canton and Jackson, Mississippi for marching and sit-ins at counters at restaurants. This civil rights movement throughout the Deep South was a cry for justice.

I also learned that three freedom riders had been killed because of the uprising. The two white freedom riders and one black: Chaney, Goodman and Schwerner were pulled from the Tallahassee River in Neshoba County, Philadelphia, Mississippi in 1964.

To me, this social awakening took place overnight because we did not have telephones nor television at that time. Local churches held meetings with the Freedom Riders and the churches were front runners in this movement. I did not know at the time that Dr. Martin Luther King, Jr., the drum major for justice, a preacher from Atlanta, was our new Moses. Like Moses, Dr. Martin Luther King had gone to the mountaintop, saw the Promised Land and got a glimpse of racial equality taking place in this country. Though unlike the first Moses, our new Moses was forced to die the tragic death of a gunshot wound in Memphis, Tennessee fighting for garbage workers (a sign of the times). Dr. King's Nonviolent philosophy adopted from Mahatma Gandhi, was effective and the Racists were sick and tired of it. The Racists were reacting violently. They conspired to dispose of him. They silenced him and for years and it seems that it worked.

Nobody else was brave enough to step up and carry out this fight for justice on the scale that he was able to do.

I have come to know that Martin Luther King, Jr. had to have courage to be out front in the fight for justice. He had to have what most do not have, the ability to move forward even when you are afraid.

During the time of the Movement, President Kennedy was assassinated. My siblings and I were able to watch the news on black and white TV at my brother's house. I was grieved over the loss of my next favorite President, who I thought embraced the Movement. My favorite President was President Eisenhower because he was in power during the time that I learned what a president was. However, this John F. Kennedy was very sociable and young. I felt that I could relate to him because he allowed black people to speak openly sometimes.

Despite all the demonstrations, the killing of Medger Evers, the three Freedom Riders: Chaney, Goodman and Schwerner, and Emmit Till (when I was five years old), I was not aware of the extent of racism in this country. I did not know that racism is a countrywide disease and that the North is no better off than the South, East and West. Nobody brought up the other areas of the country. So, I thought that racism only existed in the Deep South. I had limited knowledge of what racism was. I was more depressed about my losses and changes in relationships than I was about changes occurring around me.

I did not realize that racism is a worldwide disease until I began to tune in to World History. Well, in South Africa, it was called Apartheid. Jim Crow is the name of Racism in the Deep South. Systemic Racism occurs in the other areas of this country. Racism is everywhere. I suppose that if I had to define racism on a national scope, I would say that racism is a cancerous spirit that runs deeply in the founding of America. And this cancer has been perpetuated and spread so deeply in the hearts of the community that many have embraced it and are afraid to give it up because they will lose their privilege of believing that they are more than other citizens simply because of the color of their skin. There is more to the myth. Refusing to face the truth and accept the fact that "All men are created equal," just as the founders of the country said, embracing the lie, that some men are superior because of race has become a stronghold that has to be broken. Racism, no matter how you dice it or slice it, is a hinderance to progress, joy, love and many other good things that can take place on this earth.

Journalism is an extremely critical profession as it is needed to expose the true dealings of inequality worldwide. While we do not all speak the same language, apple seeds still produce apples and orange seeds still produce oranges. I cannot sow love and reap hate.

Embracing this stronghold of racism for two hundred forty-four years has cost this country dearly. Healing is inevitable. Reparations are needed. According to the Boston Globe, 12/03/2020, "a poll conducted in June found that half of Americans, including 39 percent of White people, today support the creation of a commission to study reparations proposals for African Americans and provide Congress with a legislative road map for restitution. HR 40, a bill first introduced to Congress in 1989 by the late Representative John Conyers of Michigan, already provides one route for such a commission to be established." Vice President Kamala Harris, during her term as Senator of California co-sponsored a bill that would study the effects of slavery and create recommendations for reparations. We cannot allow her to forget to get this bill signed into law.

I cannot figure out what happened to the step toward reparations in 1865 to give slaves 40 acres (about twice the area of Chicago's Millennium Park) and a mule. The effort was just stopped as other efforts toward equality during the reconstruction period after the Civil War. When the dreamer dies, so does the dream. I want to believe that when the dreamer President, Abraham Lincoln was killed, so was his dream killed. All dreams must have a dreamer. We oftentimes say that we want to keep Dr. Martin Luther King's Dream alive, but if we did not buy into the dream and do nothing to advance the dream, we let the dream die. Social change and advancement are a slow process. I suppose social change is dependent on the speed of the information technology of the age. With the way the speed of information is transmitted in today's world, one does not have an exceptionally long time to ponder what her action will be. Therefore, an extraordinarily strong moral code is needed to prevent one from swaying from one principle to another.

By the time I was about to enter the high school years, Daddy's financial economy changed. Since Daddy was a subsistence farmer, he fed the family and took care of all finances off the land. One day he was visited by one of my young African American teachers, who informed him that he could no longer grow cotton, corn, and other crops to feed the family. He was told that he would have to grow soybeans and allow the land to rest. Daddy was forced to give up his farming. This was a ploy for Jim Crow Law to do away with the little man in agriculture. I say this because the big plantation owners, mostly in the Delta, were able to get money to enhance their cotton crops and to gather the cotton with machines. The small farmers were able to get a small token in comparison to the plantation owners. To this day, many acres of land in the Hills of Mississippi are barren because the farmers are not allowed to grow their crops of choice.

I noticed the disappointment and that Daddy's health began to decline. There were no longer fun trips to the cotton gin. And there was no longer education in how Daddy counted money, which was different from the way we were taught to count money in school. In Daddy's system a quarter was two bits, a fifty-cent coin was four bits. A silver dollar was eight bits. The number zero was an aught or ought. Daddy said that his formal education ended in the fifth grade. However, he believed avidly in education for his offspring.

Daddy always wanted his children to have good education. He had sent his older children to schools away from home. Daddy was one hundred percent supportive of us girls as well. Daddy would buy musical instruments, band uniforms and anything else we needed to succeed in school.

It was later in life that Daddy shared with me that he had to work hard to maintain and keep his property because the KKK had fought with him because he did not sell his land to them. He talked about how they had killed his livestock and that the two property owners next to Daddy's property had tried to land lock his property. They both were Klansmen.

Daddy had to go to court to get an easement into his property. And when he won the case, he was only awarded a one-lane road into his property. So, if one vehicle were coming into the property, the other vehicle exiting the property would have to backup and allow the other vehicle access. This exercise would sometimes cause one of the drivers to back up one half a mile because our house was just that far from the main thoroughfare.

I would see Daddy sitting on the front porch sometimes with his double-barreled shotgun on his lap. I learned much later that he was experiencing Post Traumatic Stress Disorder. One of the symptoms is flashbacks. I was more understanding of why our living room wall was decorated with rifles and double-barreled shotguns.

I was later to learn that the racist tactics did not end there. When I was about ten years old, a power line was put up. The power line was about a mile from our home. But somehow, Daddy was told that he was unable to get electricity to his home because he was too far from the power line.

To empower my brother's family, Daddy bought a television and a refrigerator for his home with hopes that we could go there and use these amenities sometimes. Daddy allowed us to go to my brother's house and watch TV at leisure. We could also have icy water in the summertime. My sisters and I often visited my brother's house staying late into the night. We would walk home through the woods for about a mile and a half after watching Black and White TV to get home and get ready for school. One of my sister's favorite TV shows was "The Fugitive." I just enjoyed watching Barney Fife in the "Andy Griffith Show" and TV in general. Listening to Rock 'N Roll and the Blues on the Radio.

I recall being at my brother's house when President John F. Kennedy's Funeral Procession was held. We did not go to school that day. I grieved his death as my niece, and I stayed home from school and watched together. I felt that someone had killed the Messiah. Afterall, he was good looking and said quite a few things that I liked and took note of. One of his quotes, that I really liked is, "Now is the time for all good men to come to the aid of their country." It did not appear to me that the President was gearing up for war and that the war was going to have a significant impact on how I saw life and how life was going to change in general. I did not realize that my boyfriend would be drafted and a few of the young men that I was close to in school would lose their lives in the war. The Vietnam War was very real to me. I had a nephew to be drafted right out of high school like the other young boys were. And the only consoling words about the loss of life in the war were, "Ask not what your country can do for you; ask what you can do for your country." And "Now is the time for all good men to come to the aid of their country." I began to resent the last statement by President John F. Kennedy because I was forced to type it repeatedly in my typing class.

Knowledge & Wisdom
Are Not Equal

Leaning to my own understanding, I assumed that my parents were just taking care of their biological urges when they conceived me. I assumed that I was just another statistic that resulted from their passions. Afterall, there were already nineteen siblings between the two of them. They had four children together. I made this assumption, not realizing that God has a divine plan for all people, myself included. My thinking was shallow. I just assumed too much. I had much knowledge, but not a lot of wisdom. Rumor had it that when I was about to be born, the midwife could not deliver me like she had all my other sisters. The way the story went, Mama was transported to Jackson, Mississippi to deliver me. I was delivered a day or so later, after she was transported 55 miles from Goodman to Jackson, Mississippi. The delivery took a long time.

When I was born, Daddy did not have a car. This meant that he had to walk at least a mile to get my brother Clifton to drive Mama to Jackson to the Charity Hospital. The Midwife had done all that she could do to get me delivered.

Obviously, I was a fighter as I was delivered at a healthy weight and was not sickly. I just heard Daddy say a couple of times as I was growing up that I was a 'blue baby'. I was to learn later that blue baby syndrome is due to several conditions that affect oxygen transportation in the blood. I never noticed that I was blue, but I was easily tired once I was a teenager and was not eating a nutritional diet. Something must have been true regarding my condition that doctors later diagnosed my ailment to be anemia. I was never forced to do chores or work around the farm or the house as my sisters were. I was never even invited to do chores. I had to ask to churn milk. Otherwise, I was left with a lot of time to play and be creative.

Not having chores meant that I also had a lot of time to read and draw as a child. I became unusually creative in my playtime because I did not have toys. For example, a corn shuck on a cob after the corn kernels were removed, became a doll. I would comb the doll's hair and plat it. Sometimes I would curl the hair and imagined that the corn shuck doll was Barbie. I would curl the hair with the way I handled the comb. All my sisters and I would get dolls for Christmas. But my sister who was, two years older than me would tear her doll open to take the instrument out that made the doll cry. She taught me to take the instrument and blow in it to make sounds as if a baby was crying. Shortly after that she would cut her doll's hair off. It did not take her long to convince me to do the same. After that, the dolls were no longer useful or desirable for us to play with. This also meant that we would have to wait until the next Christmas to get a doll if my brother Daddy's youngest son who lived in Cleveland decided to send us dolls.

Much later in my life after I became an adult, Mama informed me that she would not have had any children if she had access to birth control like we do nowadays. She made it clear that when she had sex it was simply for the pleasure. I had to accept and respect her honesty when she did not deny that she liked sex. She just did not like the consequence of unprotected sex, having babies. When she was in her eighties, she told one of my sisters and me that had she had birth control when she was having children, she would not have had any of us. However, she did tell my brother when he tried to get her to tell him that she specifically loved him for one hundred dollars, "I love all of my children." She took the one hundred dollars, but never told him that she just loved him. She informed me that a woman cannot get pregnant if she does not enjoy sex. She did not waste any time telling me when I was a teenager, that I just needed to keep my dress down when I questioned her about sex. I had then, nor do I have now any reason to disbelieve her statements based on my individual experiences later. Mama did not bite her tongue and was honest when I questioned her.

I never became bitter to the point where I would disrespect her, except that one time when she had come back into our home after Daddy died to live with us. I was then a teenager, but I never stopped regretting talking back to her when one day she tried to keep me from eating a jar of preserves. I was of the mindset that she could have stayed wherever she went when she left Daddy and us. But had she not come back, we would have been in foster care. We did not have relatives that had the accommodations to take care of us and their families too. She was able to keep up appearances that she was there, although she was there to get the small social security check, cash it, buy a few groceries, give us a few dollars, and leave home again with the balance. Mama had another life, and it was not there with us girls.

I never had the opportunity to catch my parents in the act of having sex, even though I slept with them until I was almost three years old. Maybe Daddy was too tired and sick. Both were tired and sick. Daddy was sixty and Mama was forty years old when I was born. Daddy worked his farm from early morning until sundown. Mama worked around the house, cooking and cleaning. She did not work on the farm.

I remember Mama treating Daddy for boils on his stomach. She would put a thread into the sore, coil it around and snatch the core of the boil out of his stomach when the infection hardened enough a few days later. One of the sores was the size of a dime in perimeter. The other was the size of a pea. Mama would pull the string out and all the infection would come out with the string. Daddy did not go to the doctor. Mama was the doctor. She was an expert on home remedies. All the cures she could not get from The Watkin's Man, she would make on her own or purchase from the general store. Castor oil, corn shuck tea, vapor rub, you name it. She had it. I recall talk about making tea from cow dung to cure whooping cough. I was glad that I did not have whooping cough. Corn shuck tea was the remedy for the itching measles. I do not recall a remedy for chicken pox. I did have chicken pox, but not the mumps. You would know if you had mumps if your jaws swelled so large that they disfigured you. Thankfully, we had vaccinations for the childhood diseases. Had there not been vaccinations, I could have bet and made money on the fact that Mama would figure out some mixture of unpleasant ingredients for us to take.

Daddy was just too scared to go to the doctor. One time later in life Daddy had gone to the doctor to have a tooth extracted. A man died while Daddy was in the waiting room. Daddy walked out of the waiting room, went home, and tied a thread to the doorknob and then tied the string to his tooth. He sat there for a long time waiting to get his nerve up to slam the door. My older sister got fed up with the situation and slammed the door. The tooth flew out of his mouth. This solved the problem. Daddy used corn whiskey from his personal distillery to soften the pain. This is the whiskey Daddy would swear by its goodness to his customers. He survived the tooth extraction. I never heard him crying out from pain. Daddy was tough.

God Controls Life and Death

A t some point in life, you learn to question things your parents tell you. You see that some of the things that they tell you do not turn out the way that they said they would. However, I think that we all have a level of acceptance when it comes to what our parents tell us. We mostly take everything they say at face value. We do this either because we like what they say or that we are too lazy to check out the rationale. And sometimes the parents are too weary and exhausted from their physical labor to think of a more logical explanation at the time.

I learned much later in life, about 37 years later that you cannot believe everything that your mother tells you either. Mama told the sister just before me that's she and I would not have children. I accepted this, believed this to be the truth only to learn shortly thereafter that she was being sarcastic. She just had to be being sarcastic I thought later. But at the time, I was thinking that Mama knew something about our health that she had not told us.

This is my truth that I was living by when very shortly after she made the remark about our inability to have kids, my sister, who was already 40 years old became pregnant. She had an active baby boy. I soon followed in my sister's footsteps. About a year later, I delivered twins. I was thirty-nine years old when they arrived. I saw no reason not to take the risk of having unprotected sex because I was convinced that I could l not get pregnant. I was also thinking that I needed to experience what the natural penis felt like. It had been a few years since I had experienced that. Mama said that I could not get pregnant anyway. Big joke. Still being in denial, despite having cravings and morning sickness at 2 and 3pm, I was four months pregnant.

My boys and me, 1990, R. Austin, L. Justin

When Seasons Change, there is Always a Storm

I married in 1975. The marriage took place after a turbulent relationship. I had lived with him and came to learn a lot about him. But there is always more to learn during a relationship, married or not. As far as I could tell, I loved him, but I had learned to put myself first and to put him next in line. Afterall, I had learned a bit about him that I did not like when I cohabited with him for two years before marriage. After my first failed relationship with the love of my life, all others were about survival. Losing my Daddy at age 12 did not make it any better. I had to survive. I was having too many losses. I turned inward. I did not love anyone so much that I could not walk away if I needed to. It was a situation best described by a friend of mine who shared that a guy had told her, "You could take me or leave me, can't you?" So, it was no traumatic scene for me to leave him when circumstances became turbulent in College Park, Georgia. I left him in Georgia and moved to Chicago with family. I began to prosper. My fiancé later joined me in Chicago after I decided to take a phone call from him after a few months. I was able to resist him if I did not hear his voice. But once I heard his voice, I caved in. Plans were made to reconcile the relationship.

My Garden Wedding, July 19, 1975

However, it was not easy getting my fiancé to see that I was no longer the girl he knew in Georgia. He followed me to Chicago and thought that I would continue to cohabitate without my ring. I again became frustrated and gave him an ultimatum. I was able to manage on my own now. My second oldest sister and I had purchased a home in a Southside Chicago neighborhood. I was a supervisor in Bookkeeping at Borg Warner Acceptance Corporation. He came to Chicago, brought his bed and thought that he could live there without paying rent. We could use a rent-paying roommate, but not a user. Plus, it would not have been fair to charge my niece rent, and he does not contribute. I was forced to evict him. He finally got the message, moved out and produced a ring. We were married shortly thereafter.

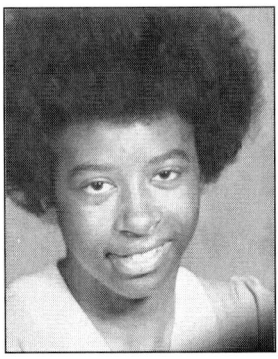

My niece and roommate.

I continued to work hard and get promotions. I became a successful Insurance Agent and Assistant Manager at The Equitable Life Assurance Company there in Chicago. And my husband was assistant manager for several prominent credit unions. He knew the business well as he was trained to manage at The Bank of Indiana because he had a cousin there, who was a Vice President and ensured that my husband was well trained.

When my husband became Vice President of United Airlines Credit Union in Chicago in the late 1970's, we began to enjoy our travel benefits and somehow grew apart. It was so subtle, but before we knew it, we had grown apart. We both traveled most weekends in different directions. We had different friends. I knew that he was traveling to the West Coast to follow his brother, who was a Tight End for the San Diego Chargers and to attend tail gate parties. My husband loved himself some football. He had played for the Missouri Tigers in College and had his shoulder dislocated by the late Gale Sayers. For some reason, my husband's college career was aborted before he could graduate, and he ended up in Indiana with his father and his wife.

My husband was living in his father's house. When I graduated from Tougaloo College, he picked me up from my graduation and we went to live in Atlanta, Georgia on that very day. I had fallen in love with him from talking extensively on the phone. I visited him once when I was on Spring Break at his father's house in Michigan City, Indiana. The family liked me right away. I liked them too. He had aunts my age. They liked to party.

Although I did not like to party much, this let me know the family was cool and nonjudgmental.

With his banking skills, my husband had no difficulty finding work in his field. He had a pattern of job hopping for more money every two years if he was not promoted. He landed a job with United Airlines Credit Union. I was excited about the flying benefits package of $10,000. I took advantage of them. I even planned a trip to the French Riviera. I had been rolling along in life, leaning to my own understanding about truth without acknowledging nor realizing that my life was being steered by a force much greater than myself. Something had come between my husband and me that I could not put my finger on. I noticed that I was traveling to different cities than he. He mostly visited Los Angeles or wherever his brother was playing football with the Chargers Team. He began to cultivate different friends than mine.

My marriage dissolved when my husband saw the need to move to Los Angeles. He told me that he wanted to live closer to his biological mother there. I thought it unusual, but I could not figure out the situation until I got into it. My husband had moved on with his life and I was not really a part of it. Yet, he was too polite to tell me. I was too immature to face reality and he was nice enough to allow me to tag along, despite his attempt to leave me alone in the house in the Chicago Suburbs.

He lost his job with United Airlines. He told me that he would look for work in Los Angeles. He tried to convince me to stay in Illinois. I would not listen. All the signs were there. This relationship was drastically changing. One day, I went to the front door, opened it and not one, but three foreclosure notices fell off. I took the foreclosure notices and gave them to him. He had asked me to take care of the bills one day and I refused. I mistakenly thought that it was the man's job to take care of the bills. My daddy did. Now, I was regretting that I had not decided to do this. My logic was that if my husband was hooked on drugs, and I was handling the money and refused to give him the household expense money, he would physically harm me. We had moved far out west of Chicago. My family was nowhere near there. So, I was off to Los Angeles. Afterall, it was all about me. I was a survivor.

I could see the deterioration in my marriage once I was living in Los Angeles. As a matter of fact, I already knew that my marriage was on the rocks, but I could not figure it out. Afterall, he was not being abusive. I just found myself spending a large amount of time alone when we should have been having fun together as we did in Chicago. It was also in Los Angeles that I realized that my husband was no longer interested in marriage. The sex life, the glue no longer existed. I began to have thoughts that there was another woman, but I could never catch him with one. He was exceedingly popular, but always came home nights. Two years later, I saw the evidence that it was time for me to dissolve the marriage because my spouse was putting the marriage second to his social life. I moved into a studio apartment, which was all that I could afford. He moved into a nice one bedroom apartment. It was better than the one we moved away from.

I had left my job with Internal Revenue Service (IRS) as a Revenue Officer and went to work for Los Angeles Police (LAPD) in Communications. I left IRS merely because they paid less than LAPD. I had difficulty adjusting to the job in the position of Dispatcher. I had moved out from my spouse. I became paranoid, and I could not adjust to the physical plant, which was nine levels below the ground with no windows. Nor was I able to adjust to the rotating shifts. I decided to quit before I was fired. This was when I told my husband that I was going to Jackson, MS to visit my mother for a while. Really, I had no intention of going back to Los Angeles if I could get out alive.

I am not certain that I became paranoid about Los Angeles because of the high crime and hearing the horror stories on the dispatch radio or was it that I had no relatives there that I knew of? I was informed by the Late Jackie Robinson's Aunt, who lived behind our apartment building across the walkway that she knew that there was a Ragland living in Los Angeles and that she attended some of the parties that Jackie's aunt attended. Unfortunately, I left the apartment before meeting this Ragland that she knew.

I recall the sessions where the employees would be scared straight at LAPD. I had joined a fraternity. There was to be no partying with others outside the fraternity. If an employee would be found at a party where there were drugs, whether or not the employee was doing drugs, she would be fired because of being at the party location. I also remember tales of how the police were so hated by the citizens that the workers in communications would be targeted and killed just because they were associated with the police.

On another occasion the Watch Commander warned the workers to stop sending 'To Messages' to the officers in the cars on Friday because somebody was going to get hurt and when we came to work on Monday, we got the news that an officer and his wife were playing with a gun and the gun went off, killing the male officer. It did not help that I came to know of the Detective, who was raping Communication Service Representatives (CSR) all on the second floors and up in their apartment buildings. His wife led the police to his arrest by sharing his Modus Operandi when he had sex with her.

And then, the Olympics were coming to Los Angeles. We CSR's were informed that the Communications Center was a target for bombings and there were terrorists in the Middle East who could make a bomb in their kitchens, that would penetrate the walls of the Communications Center. If the Communications Center would be bombed, all human life would be killed and only the paperwork would be saved by the 40,000 of halogen gas placed there to protect the history of Los Angeles.

As if this was not enough, Marvin Gaye was killed, and I happened to be working the emergency line on that Sunday Morning. I took the call from a citizen, who appeared to be deranged. But he was telling the truth. The anonymous caller informed me that if I did not believe him that I should go across the street to the Parker Center Jail and see that Marvin's father was locked up there.

This is the moment that I decided that it was not worth the trauma to work for LAPD in any role. I left the job and the city.

I had already moved out from my husband. Needless to say, I do not think that he cared that I was leaving. He would now have some time to think things out. I knew that he would never come clean with me about his addiction. God had to show me that he was dealing with this issue. I first read an article in Ebony Magazine by Smokey Robinson. On another occasion, a coworker at IRS told me that he saw my husband at the candy store. This comment went right over my head. I assumed that the coworker was trying to say that he saw him at the Comedy Store in Hollywood. It took an act of God to have me go to the car registered in my name to find the evidence on the dashboard of a convertible vehicle in front of our apartment building on the street. I say it was God because I would never have gone to the mailbox at 5 PM while a female neighbor was visiting. I went to the car to put the top on it when I saw the evidence. Being ignorant of the contents of the ashtray, the little metal pipe and a small vial, I carried them upstairs on the elevator with other residents out in the open. I was unaware of what the stares of the other residents on the elevator were, I walked into the apartment with the evidence. My neighbor could not wait to light it up and try it. My husband's face revealed to me that he was guilty although he blamed his little brother, who could not drive my car. I was petrified. I was also very much afraid now that I had confirmed that this was the reason for his severe depression and that it was not clinical. This is when I informed him that I was moving away from him and that he needed to get himself to rehabilitation. I suppose he saw no reason to explain anything now that I knew. This was one of the conversations that we should have had, but never did.

I went home to Mama to learn that I could not live with her and moved out on my own. I was in my mid-30's. This is when I learned that I would not be able to live in Mississippi and work for an insurance company. I got a firsthand revelation about race relations in Mississippi. Mississippi is still and always has been the White Man's Paradise. He rules all. He has all power there. I was in for a rude awakening. My personality was not a good fit, although I was born and raised there. I was not covered, and I was more educated than the managers that I worked for. The black community had no fight in them. They stayed in their lane. I needed to shut up or get out of Dodge. I reluctantly conceded. I had a Rhema Word from my sister and my niece, who came to visit from St. Louis. They felt that I needed to move out of Mississippi, move to St. Louis and open a beauty salon with my sister. I packed my bags.

It was when I moved to St. Louis in 1986 that I realized another seasonal change. A storm was on the horizon. This storm was going to change my life forever. I recall saying to myself that St. Louis was an okay place to visit, but I would never want to live there. Afterall, St. Louis had changed socially in a tremendous way over the last decade and it was not positive change. There was a large amount of crime in the city and places that I liked to frequent were no longer in business. I wondered, what happened to Chop Suey? I referred primarily to Gas Light Square, where had it gone? Where was my boyfriend in St. Louis, who had graduated from Beaumont years ago? He was probably married. He was too nice not to be married.

Despite my negative feelings about St. Louis, I rationalized that since two of my favorite people lived there. I could make St. Louis my next move because Jackson, MS was not looking safe to me. I realized that would need to have the covering of my husband to successfully live there as an attractive single female. There is safety in numbers. I would move with relatives that I had a closer bond with. I never recall stopping and asking for the counsel of God. It was all about me. I truly believed that I was in charge and control of my life.

I never dreamed that I would be trying to live in this new St. Louis, which now had few of the fun places that I frequented when I visited as a child. My sister and I would open a beauty salon in St. Louis. We did everything except that. She worked out of her home. She had her son in 1987. I went to beauty school to get a license and had my twins in 1988. Our beauty salon together never happened.

I could move to St. Louis and go into the Beauty Salon Business with my sister, I thought. All I must do is get a Cosmetology license. I already knew how to do hairdressing as I had been pressing and marcel ironing people's hair since age 7.

Before I moved to St. Louis, I had never heard voices before. I had once had a very convincing negative thought about what my husband was doing in Los Angeles. But one day when I was home alone in St. Louis, I heard a very clear audible voice speak to me, "Girl, you are really working too hard. You are going to school and working. You only have yourself to care for. Now if you got yourself a Sugarman, he could take care of you while you go to school." I thought, that is a good thing. That is what I will do. I then packed the thought away and went on living. One Sunday my niece and I went to church. When we went through the receiving line at the end of service, I noticed that one of the preachers was so glad to see me, he jumped line in the receiving line and told the other preacher, "Get back, this one is mine." It never occurred to me that I would be getting a phone call later that week with an offer to go to lunch. We did that one Sunday when it was snowing. My niece and her paramour warned me not to go to lunch with him. I went to lunch anyway and I was propositioned. Remembering the voice that I heard, this was my confirmation. This was my Sugar Daddy. I said, "Yes" after being so nervous that I had to go to the restroom and twirl around a few times as I was so elated about the proposition. Frankly, I had assumed that he fit the bill for being a Sugar Daddy as he was much older than me and I assumed that he was no good in the bed. He would just be a bread ticket.

Was I in for a big surprise? I saw him at my home a few times and we began to have sex. We always used condoms. I soon began to miss him very much when there were holidays. I felt that I had to always have him around me. This was not likely. He was not mine.

A few months later, I moved away from my niece and went to live with my sister, in St. Louis City and her husband. Shortly after moving with my sister, and soon moving out, after we had an altercation because I was seeing the Sugar Daddy, I again heard an audible voice which said to me, "Girl, you have not had the real thing for years. You would probably really like it if you did it without the condom." Again, I gave in to the voice. It made so much sense to me. The next time we had sex, I told him to take the condom off halfway the session.

I did not believe it when the gynecologist diagnosed my pregnancy. Although he was one of St. Louis' finest, a graduate of Homer G. Hospital, now closed, I doubted him. Had not Mama told me that I could not have children, I might have believed the doctor's report. I decided that the doctor had to be in error. Afterall, the doctor had to do a test and call me later and tell me, "Ms. Coleman you are pregnant, and you are so far along." Mama had told me that I could not have children. Or did she say, "You and Barb would not have children?" Afterall, I had only had sex without a condom that one time. So, I could not be pregnant. The sex was the greatest I had ever had, just like the voice had said to me and just like Mama had said, "You can't get pregnant if you do not enjoy the sex." The audible voice had told me, "Girl, you haven't had the real thing since you don't know when." I could not be pregnant because I could not get pregnant, per Mama. "That settles it," I reasoned to myself.

I did not associate the unsettled feelings I had around two and three o'clock in the afternoon with what pregnant women call morning sickness. Afterall, I was not getting sick in the morning. Neither did I associate the fact that although I did not care for pickles, whenever I drove past White Castle, I found myself turning around and going there to buy cheeseburgers for the taste of pickles and mustard. I did not connect the fact that whenever I ate eggs, I vomited them up and that that was morning sickness. Frankly speaking, the only time I had been sick in the morning was Easter Sunday Morning, which prompted me to go see the doctor on Monday. I was extremely sick but had no pain anywhere. I was just depressed, and I was so nauseated that I got out of the bed and laid on the floor. I was on program at church that afternoon, but I could not see myself going to church this day. I was just too sick to do so.

I called the Pastor and informed him that I would not be able to come to church that day. As I was lying on the floor, I felt a fluttering in my abdomen. I was going to the doctor to rule out sexually transmitted disease. I just knew that was what was wrong with me.

On Monday, I was able to get an appointment. I was first ignorant of the fact that I was pregnant. The doctor examined me and turned to leave the treatment area, which was separated by a room divider, and said, "I will tell you how far along you are when I get back." I was thinking that he was talking to someone else next door to me. Afterall, pregnancy was the farthest thing from my mind. I was thinking that it was tacky for the doctor to be seeing two patients at the same time. The doctor came back and told me, "Yes, I did find a trace of trichomoniasis, but that can be cleared up pretty easy. The other thing is that you are 14 weeks (about 3 months) pregnant." The doctor gave me my prescription for the sexually transmitted disease. I left the clinic unconvinced that I was pregnant.

Taking my time about it, I went to get an ultrasound just to prove the doctor wrong. I had a plan. I would get an ultrasound. I was in awe. The doctor had to be wrong. Mama said I could not get pregnant, so I wasn't pregnant, and I had only had sex one time without a condom. I was also prepared to blast my partner because obviously he was having sex with other nasty women. When I looked up the definition of Trichomoniasis I learned that this sexually transmitted infection is caused by a parasite. Is among the most common sexually transmitted infections. Trichomoniasis's risk factors include multiple sexual partners and not using condoms during sex. Trichomoniasis causes a rank vaginal discharge, genital itching, and painful urination in women. Men typically have no symptoms. Complications include a risk of premature delivery for pregnant women. Treatment involves both partners taking one large dose of a certain oral antibiotic. There was no prescription to be had for pregnant out of wedlock women. Missing periods did not phase me because I was irregular, just like my sister, who got pregnant last year. She did not learn that she was pregnant until she was eight months pregnant. I was just almost four months along, hah.

I walked into the abortion clinic to get my ultrasound. I was a bit arrogant, looking down on the other patients there because I was not pregnant and was not getting an abortion. I just needed to have documentation that the doctor's diagnosis was incorrect. In 1988, the patient was forced to ingest large amounts of water before the test is given. I drank my water and followed instructions. When I was on the table getting the test, the technician kept sighing and saying in a faint voice, "Hmmm, sounds like two." I was still in denial.

When I was called for consultation, the lady said, "Ms. Coleman, it appears that you are having multiple births and you are too far along to have your abortion here. You would have to go to Cape Girardeau. Do you have someone to drive you there? You may not go alone." I became unnerved at once when the clinician said, 'multiple-births'. Jumping out of my seat, I screamed loudly, "Multiple? How multiple?" I was thinking three, four. I took the pamphlets the clinician gave me and dashed out the door. I was in shock. How could I be pregnant? What would I tell my family? I was acting like a teenager. I had embraced the fake myth that I was a goody two shoes. I knew that my family thought of me as such. And it did cause a lot of chaos when they found out that I was pregnant. However, in the end, the family was more supportive. The babies were too cute to resist. My family were there for whatever I needed whether it was babysitting or anything else that involved the care of the twins. But I would have to work. Working in a Beauty Salon was not going to feed two boys. I had to put my bachelor's degree to work.

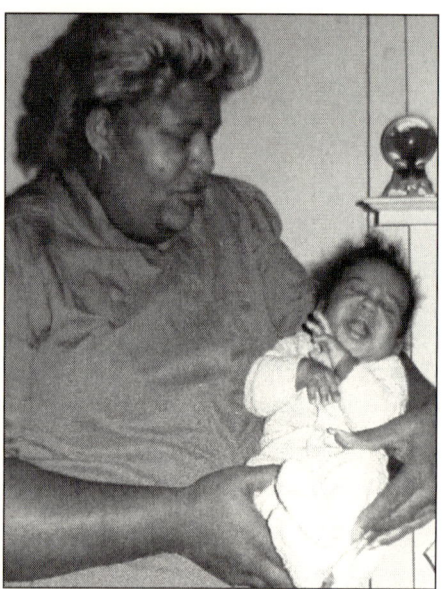

L-R My sister & her son 1987 at age 40

The doctors assigned me to a high-risk clinic because I was what the obstetrician described as 'too old to be having my first delivery.' He said that the babies could have down syndrome. The delivery was long and tedious. I gleaned from the experience that God manages life and death. I now know that God is in control. God regulated my mind and frankly all my other circumstances. I had a lot of pride. I could have been suicidal. This pregnancy was a big shock to me. As I progressed along in the pregnancy, I continued to work. I also began to look forward to having twins. It was a long ordeal. But thank God my two boys were healthy.

I went into labor at 6 pm one day and the twins were born the next day at 3:00 and 3:30 pm respectively. When Justin entered the world a natural birth, the doctors feared that Austin would have to be a Caesarian birth because he switched from headfirst to bottom first. The doctor was not having that and was able to get him turned back around to headfirst position. During this thirty-minute ordeal, Justin was being held with his hands and feet together to keep him from finding out that Austin had not arrived. Although the doctors had bonded Justin with me upon arrival, they bonded Austin with Justin and then bonded Austin with me. I thought that this was unusual but was too tired to fight at the time.

During labor, I was in deep pain and started begging for pain medication. The attending Ob-Gyn asked me what I was going to name the babies. When I told him that I was going to name one of them Anthony, he said, "Anthony sounds gay. Do not name the baby that. I will give you pain medicine if you don't name the baby Anthony." I said, "Okay, I won't name him Anthony. Now will you give me the medicine?" I do not recall receiving any medication. I fell asleep.

I do remember going into deep sleep sometime during the wee hours of the morning. I experienced the lowest of lows. I recall reciting Psalm 23, "Yeah though I walk through the valley of the shadow of death, I will fear no evil." I was so depressed! Lamaze classes did not prepare me for this part of labor. However, the breathing and pushing exercises came in very handy. Although my sister, my coach was grateful for the pushing practice. She told me that her gym membership paid off well, too. She was exhausted after the 30-minute ordeal.

I did not realize how overwhelmed with my bundles of joy until one time we were shopping for baby clothes when the twins were about nine months old. I had them in Sears in their stroller with one in the front and the other in the back. They were a team. As I was looking for clothes, they were busy walking the stroller across the floor and I was not paying attention to them. I was focused on finding outfits that were alike. When I looked up and did not see them, I panicked. I ran to Customer Service and asked her to get on the intercom and announce the twins missing. As I ran around the store looking for my babies, a man came to me and placed his hand on my shoulder. As I acknowledged him, he gently said, "Mama, don't worry about them. They will turn up. People don't kidnap poor kids." I was flabbergasted, trying to digest what the man said and not seeing my kids, I was shocked back to sanity. The twins were found on the opposite side of the store, which was about the size of a short city block. This was my insight that they had outgrown the stroller as their feet could touch the floor.

Shenanigans with My Niece

I did not escape getting my nickname, 'Jakey Boy.' I was a Tomboy during my early and pre-teen years. Much of my Tomboy experience came from my two-year stay with my niece when I was almost three years old. She is two months older than me. We spent our days climbing trees, fishing with bamboo poles, wandering, and cutting our hair with her dad's clippers. We actually acted like Tom Sawyer. We were not supervised. We were free to roam.

My niece's mother was also my sister-in-law. She kept herself busy around the house and working in the garden, but never too far out of eyesight. However, she was never able to catch us at our mischief. My Sister-In-Law was never quick to give a child corporal punishment as Mama was. She appealed to our consciousnesses. Little did she know, we did not have consciousnesses. We tried whatever appealed to us at the time. Had she been as merciless as Mama, I would have tried to talk my niece out of many of the devilish acts we engaged in.

My Sister-in-Law thought that girls should look like girls. She would dress us in dresses when we got up mornings and by noon, she would find herself having to sew our dresses back on the waists. We had no idea what acting lady like was. My Sister-in-Law would fuss a little and sew us back up. Off we were to do the same thing again, rip our dresses off their waists.

Dress tails had a great function of holding the blackberries that we picked. All the berries that we did not eat, we took them home to cook.

Sometimes there were enough for a blackberry cobbler. We would also collect nuts from hickory nut trees. Of course, our dress tails served as our baskets for carrying the nuts as well.

Cutting our hair with the clippers was one of the most memorable shenanigans we girls engaged in. Both of us have the scars from that to this day. She cut my hair on each side of my bangs, and I cut her top braid off.

My Sister-in-Law was working in the garden when we decided to become barbers. The barber, my brother Clifton had left his clippers in plain sight of us and left home. It was customary for the men to cut hair in the front yard.

My niece and I took advantage of the opportunity to cut our hair. The clippers were easy enough for us to maneuver.

Sister-in-Law came home and saw us. She was too embarrassed to allow us to walk with her to church, about a country block away, even though it was getting dark.

When My niece and I finally did show up at church, everybody looked at us and gasped. We were the main attraction of the hour. We got many gazes and stares of unbelief from everyone in the congregation. We just sat there in shock as if we did not know what the big deal was. We really got the message that we had messed up and somehow, we survived the ordeal and remembered not to cut our hair again.

Our hair grew back over time. However, the hair grew back with a different texture and length. We were repeatedly scolded by Sister-in-Law because she did not know what to do about My niece's missing top braid. Her only alternative was to tie a ribbon in the top of her head to make it look like she had hair. My niece looked very much like Winnie the Pooh, the comic strip character.

Although I had later moved back home with Daddy and my sisters, I still would visit my niece at her home and was always accepted with open arms. Daddy's kids and his son Clifton and my Sister-in-Law's kids were so close in age and bloodline that there was an unquestionable and natural bond. It was a few years later that my niece and I engaged in a life-changing shenanigan.

The next shenanigan we engaged in was finding condoms in the master bedroom dresser drawer. We were ecstatic that we had found these balloons. We blew them up and some of them burst. Then we put water in others as we blew them up. Had we known the purpose of these balloons were, we might have done things differently.

It was not long after blowing up the balloons that my niece got a little sister that we had to babysit while everybody else was in the cottonfields. She was seven years younger than my niece and six years younger than me. It appears that the cost of the condoms was too expensive, or my niece's parents just decided that they were not worth the effort. I say this because about a year after the birth of my niece's sister, we witnessed the birth of a brother two years later and two years later, the birth of another baby boy. It seemed that they just threw up their hands and spontaneously made passionate love. In the end, my brother and my sister-in-law had six children.

My six closest nieces and nephews at the youngest niece's wedding.

My playmate-niece's grad photo 1967

After a two-year stint of living with My niece and her family, my niece, my playmate got away from me. She started to go to school, and I went back home to live with my sisters and Daddy. My niece started going to school a year before I did because of her birthdate. Although she was just two months older than me, she was able to go to school one year before me. Having to separate from My niece was heartbreaking for me. When I reflect on all the dangerous tomboy-acts we were involved in, both of us were lucky to be alive to see this day. I no longer had a playmate my age during the day. Daddy was my companion until my sisters came home from school. He was smart enough not to leave me alone. I went every-where he went before the other kids were home. We went to the cotton gin, shopped in downtown Goodman, visited some of the other property owners whose land was close to ours. And sometimes he would hitch the mules to the wagon and drive me about two miles over a one lane road to his cousin's house. Daddy would not tell me when we were taking this route because he knew that I was afraid to ride along the large crater that looked like the Grand Canyon on one of the neighboring properties. The road had eroded, and a tree blocked his ability to drive around the crater. The only choice Daddy had was to make the mules jump over the break in the road past the tree. This really scared me.

When Daddy took me shopping in Goodman for shoes, I made it a point to let him and the storeowner know that I liked patent leather shoes and not the brogans which we called 'hi-tops' then and now they are very expensive Timberlands. I wanted the patent leather shoes so badly that I convinced Daddy that I could wear the first pair that I could force my foot into. I wore the shoes home. When I got home, I had blisters on my feet. My feet got bigger, and I could no longer wear them.

After the incident with trying to press my hair, I was off to live with my niece and her family for a couple of years. I was shocked to know that Daddy and I would no longer be hanging out every day. I was learning from Daddy how to make cornbread in a skillet on the fireplace and hoe cakes on the kitchen stove. There was none of the fancy biscuits, cakes and pies that Mama cooked. Daddy's favorite pot was the Dutch oven. He could cook almost anything in it.

As I look back at the dangerous activities that my niece and I engaged in, it was probably a great benefit to mankind that we were separated for a period. We were so sheltered and free to roam around my niece's 40-acre farm that we did not understand that this unleashed freedom comes with a huge amount of responsibility.

I did not know why, but I found out later that my three older sisters, had tired of living up the hill from my niece with my married older sister, because she was a 'glutton' for punishment of kids. My older sister and her husband did not have kids, although they had raised two. I did not see my other three sisters much for the two years we lived apart. I was not aware that they were receiving harsh treatment by my older sister. However, it is believable because once I remember riding to church with my older sister and her husband and she was extremely strict about the way I had to behave in the car. I would have feelings of suffocation sitting on the backseat. This is called motion sickness. I would stand up as there were no seatbelt laws in those days. This older sister would yell at me to sit still and not move. She otherwise had no conversation for me.

I also recall Daddy leaving me with my older sister a couple of times and she would cook an egg for me for breakfast. The only thing she would ask me was how did I like my egg. I told her to turn it over. She would stare at me as if she were trying to figure me out as I ate. I ate alone and in silence noticing that my older sister was soon off to her housework. Shortly thereafter she would have a visitor, either a man named Sam Johnson and sometimes, her Pastor.

My older sister was an Eastern Star, and she was exceedingly popular. She often had visitors, mostly males. I had learned early on from Mama that I was not to get in grown folks' business. I would spend time on the back porch until Daddy came and took me home.

Daddy's Humor

Daddy had a gigantic sense of humor. We did not see this side of him too often, but we saw it often enough.

One of the most hilarious things Daddy taught us was that there was no Santa Claus. Daddy had bought our Christmas fruit and other things and put them in a closet to hide them from us until Christmas Day. My sisters and I could smell the Washington State Apples. The odor permeated throughout the room. The oldest of us went into the closet, took out one of the apples and shared it with the rest of us. Somehow, Daddy found out that we had tampered with the fruit.

Daddy called the four of us together and said, "Alright. I just wanted to tell y'all that there is no such thing as Santa Claus. No there's no damned Santa Claus." I was devastated! All the other girls looked disappointed. We knew that Daddy was on to our game of stealing the fruit.

On another occasion, we knew that Daddy was going hunting. We convinced him to take us hunting with him. I was pierced in the eye by a pine needle at once as we ventured into the woods. I started whining. Daddy escorted us back home and we awakened the next morning to find that Daddy had gone hunting after we went to sleep and that he had caught a raccoon.

Daddy rarely left us home alone and ventured far off. This particular morning Daddy told us that he was going to town and that we were to hoe a section of the cottonfield directly down the hill from our house.

The oldest of the four of us had found Daddy's corn whiskey. She had no idea that this was the fifth of whiskey that Daddy had planned to sell to his cousin. She gave each of us girls some whiskey in a teacup and put sugar and water in it for us to drink. I do not think that she put any water and sugar in hers because she got drunk.

The three younger ones of us had gone to the house because the sun was too hot in July in Mississippi around Noon. We did not notice that the oldest of the four of us had not left the cottonfield.

Daddy came home and asked about her whereabouts. We went looking for her and found her in the cottonfield passed out in the hot sun. She had parked her hoe where it could stand up and mark where she stopped chopping cotton. Her body was nearby. Somehow, we were able to revive her and get her into the house out of the sun without much of a fight.

Later in the day, a cousin came by to buy the whiskey from Daddy that my sister had stolen. Daddy gave him a taste of the whiskey. His cousin spat out the whiskey and said, "Cousin Buster, something is wrong with this whiskey." Daddy said, "You're lying, man. I know that this is damn good whiskey because I made it myself." Daddy then took a drink and was appalled. Daddy's facial expression let us know that he had found out that oldest sister had stolen his whiskey and had filled the bottle back up with water.

Knowing that we were not to drink whiskey, we were sneaking around watching as we kept all of Daddy's visitors under strict surveillance. This time we knew we had a whipping coming. Not knowing that he would not take revenge right away, we put on all the few clothes we had to keep the belt from stinging so badly. We were miserable and hot in July with all our clothes on. Daddy knew we had a trick going. He would look at us out of the side of his eyes and I could see he was tickled.

Daddy did not whip us this day. He waited for about four days later when the oldest of the four of us did something else wrong and caused us to have to line up for punishment.

I was never whipped by Daddy because I learned early on that the sooner you cry, the sooner he would stop the 'lashings of his belt.' The oldest of the four of us was a great dancer and would cry loudly. She would get a few lashings before being let go. The second oldest of the four of us could not cry. She got a few lashings more because of it. The third oldest learned to cry and would get a couple of lashings. I knew I did not want a lashing and I would start sobbing loudly before he started the punishment on anyone. When my turn came, I would get a lecture and Daddy would warn my sisters against getting me in trouble. He called me "My Baby."

We should have known that the punishment would not be too severe because Daddy was tired and overweight. He administered the punishments from a seated position, unlike Mama who stood up. But we had seen Daddy whipping his farm animals and the neighborhood boy that he cared for because he would steal molasses and drink them by the gallon. It was terrifying to watch those incidents. Watching him whip the boy was enough to convince me that I did not need to get a whipping from Daddy.

I enjoyed hanging out with Daddy while he carried out the obligations of running his farm. Fun things included going to the cotton gin in Goodman with a bail of cotton, shopping at a couple of the general stores in Goodman and making groceries at J.M. Ward's Country Store. J. M. Ward's store was closer to our home than Goodman. We usually walked to J. M. Wards' and rode in my brother's truck to the cotton gin in Goodman. Goodman was about thirteen miles from our farm.

One day at J.M. Ward's store, Daddy saw an older man getting ready to drop a B.C. Powder, a potent headache drug into an RC Cola. Daddy said, "Hey, I wouldn't do that if I were you, man." The older man did not listen. He was pouring the B.C. Powder into the drink and instantly created a bomb. All of the solution flew out of the bottle past the older man's ear. He was in total shock after the incident. He forgot that he had a headache. Daddy told him, "The next time you take that, put the powder in your mouth and then drink the RC slowly. When Daddy learned that the man had used all of his allowance to buy the BC and the Cola, Daddy was generous and bought him more. The man was more successful doing it Daddy's way.

Daddy would take me to Allen Dunn's General Store. Allen Dunn was a white man. Allen was very cordial with Daddy and enjoyed playing with me. Allen sold shoes and dresses. I would be dressed in overalls with a plaid shirt. My shoes were on the style of what we now call Timberland's. Back then, they were referred to as High-tops or Clod Knockers. I would go into the store dressed like a little boy and would come out dressed like a princess because Allen had convinced Daddy to buy girlie things for me. I would be very excited after the shopping spree. After Allen would get Daddy to buy things for me, Allen would begin to tell me that he was my cousin and how pretty I was. This would upset Daddy and he would grab me by the hand, snatch me away from Allen and tell Allen, "I have told you not to be telling that s—t' to my children." I learned much later in life that Allen was a Jew and that he was claiming to be a relative of Daddy's.

When it was time to pay for his goods, Allen would always tell Daddy the price. Daddy would ask," What was the difference for, Allen? I figured a different amount." Allen would say, "That's because the difference is tax, Buster." Daddy would say, "Ah hell, I don't pay no damn taxes." Daddy would then snatch me by the hand, towing the package and storm out of the store. Daddy would pay what he had calculated and no more was to be added to that amount. Allen would have to eat the difference. Allen did not call the sheriff. He just let it go. I came to know later that Daddy was out of compliance. Everybody pays sales tax. It is funny and ironic to me now. Daddy would probably get hurt pulling this act in today's time. However, I figure that although the families were rural and lived miles apart, there was a cohesion and a bond of community.

I had to go to a Family Reunion to learn that research about my Daddy's family tree revealed that the first of the Raglin's to come to Mississippi was a man by the name of Robert Raglin. I also learned that Robert Raglin was Daddy's Paternal Grandfather and that he was of Jewish Origin. Also, while growing up, I came to know that the horns used around the farm that Daddy used to call his farm animals were Jewish Instruments: Shofars. The animals would respond well to the blowing of the Shofar. I also observed that there were several laying around where the cows and the mules grazed. I cannot help but wonder if Daddy brought some of his Jewish Heritage along with his Native American Heritage. Daddy's mother was Native American. Daddy did not talk much about the Native Americans either. I also have yet to learn why Daddy was so adamant that his children do not know that there was Jewish Blood in his family.

As I became a preteen, I learned that I could do acts that would make others laugh. I would role play imaginary characters. The comedy earned me the nickname. The character was risk taking and caused my sisters and friends to think of Jakey Boy as a brave soul. They admired me. I loved the attention and would perform for them for hours. I would make up the act as I saw fit. They never tired of the acting that I was doing. I believe I picked up my sense of humor from Daddy.

Daddy taught me about himself when we would sit on the front porch at night and chat. Daddy would chat and I would ask questions, none of which he did not answer. Daddy talked with me as if I was his buddy. Daddy would tell me about his lawsuit with his second wife, who was a schoolteacher. According to Daddy she had filed for a divorce and that she wanted alimony and land. Although Daddy had told me that he was afraid of his brother-in-law, he hired a Jewish lawyer, and the wife lost the case.

Daddy was brave and invincible in my opinion. Daddy said there were only two men in the world that he was afraid of, and that-his brother-in-law had gone to prison for some unpleasant crime was one of them. Daddy also said that he was afraid of another man who had gone to prison for killing his wife and preserving her genitalia in a jar. Daddy said that he had put her private parts in a jar and was keeping it in his house.

I later wondered how afraid Daddy really was of man who had done this disgusting act. I learned that this man owned one of the adjacent properties to Daddy's. I was privy to seeing this scary man one day when Daddy and the man were feuding about a woman that Daddy thought he wanted to marry. I was playing alone in our back yard one day when this man rode across Daddy's backyard on his grey Clydesdale horse. He was dressed immaculately in a black suit, dress shoes, and a black Fedora Stetson hat. I had no idea that Daddy had gone ahead of Ike to the woman's house to scare Ike away.

I have no idea what the woman saw in Daddy because he never wore a suit and did not have a Clydesdale Horse. Daddy had one mule that he could ride and that was Old Kate. Old Kate was a pretty red. But Daddy rarely rode his mules. He saved them for plowing and pulling his wagon for transportation. Daddy's dress clothes primarily consisted of light khakis and a short sleeved white shirt. I rarely saw him in a suit. Nevertheless, Daddy came out the victor and was able to continue his relationship with the woman.

We let Daddy know that we adamantly did not want this woman to be our mama and that he had put his life on the line for nothing. She already had teenage sons and daughters older than we were. Although this union did not take place, it did not stop Daddy from trying to find us a mother. On another occasion, Daddy invited a nurse to our home, just before he died. We had to let him know that she would not be able to live there either because we would not allow any woman to come into the home and that we could manage ourselves. We were not seeing Daddy as the very sick man that he was and that he would not be with us long.

Amazingly enough, Mama got the word that Daddy was about to die. She came to visit when I was about eleven years old. She began to spend the night and share his bed. She began to take care of him on his sick bed. He was very happy to have her back. He appeared to be recovering, when one day, around my twelfth birthday he succumbed to death.

Daddy was determined to find us a mother. I recall that shortly after the incident and show down over the woman, Daddy became ill and was hospitalized for a week or so. Daddy met a nurse at the hospital that he was so infatuated with, he invited her to visit him at his house. The woman was attractive and nice enough. We just did not think that we needed a mother after all of these years without one. We never thought that Daddy would end up dying and that we could end up in foster care because all of us were minors. When Daddy told us that he was thinking of marrying the nurse, my oldest sisters The oldest of the four of us and the second oldest of the four of us asked him, "Where is she going to live?" "We don't need a mama now." We never considered that Daddy just could have been lonely.

He never went out on dates that we knew of. He was very handsome. He did not seem to care one way or the other. If he was dating, he did it when we were at school. None of us girls seemed to care that Daddy needed love from the opposite sex. We could only see that he needed to be there with us. This was our truth, and we would have it no other way.

I thrived and formulated a truth that I lived by, thinking it was 'truth.' This philosophy based on rationalization and experience was "my truth." It was going to be years before I would find that what I thought most of my life was truth, when I was so wrong and distorted in my thinking. There is no alternative truth. I came to know that the truth that I was standing on was partly based on my own experiences, observations, and that of what older relatives and friends had been instilled in me as a child.

Most of what I learned from older friends, family and Sunday School lined up with what I now have embraced to be genuine truth. Yet there was a huge gap in my connotation of what was genuine truth. My thinking did not always line up with truth. I had really missed the mark when it came to morality. I was swimming in unchartered waters, yielding to my flesh. My conscience had become so traumatized along the way that I did not consider the fact that I was hurting so many others when I gave in to my physical and emotional whims. It was all about me. I was so caught up with my selfish desires to survive at any cost that I had not weighed the cost of wandering too far out into the deep.

There are many ways that I can now see that God must have had me shielded from hurt, harm and danger. Based on the outcome of many of the immoral acts that I performed over time, I was always protected. Knowing much better now, I sometimes get chills when I reflect on those times. Afterall, it was about survival then.

Sex Can Be Over-rated

There were years where I leaned to my own understanding and until my acts of immorality caught up with me, I was operating on my belief in my world view. My world view was that if you can do the wrong thing and get away with it, there were no repercussions. Isn't this what everybody else was doing in my life? Mama was attracted to Daddy's nephew. My sister's husband was having an affair with my cousin's wife. I saw these things before my parents separated. Daddy told me about a time that he had betrayed a friend by sleeping with his wife when he was in between wives. Daddy was married twice before his marriage to Mama. I was the tender age of 7 when he told me this and I wonder why he told me to this day.

Daddy shared that he met the friend's wife in the wooded area nearby her house. He tied his mule to a tree and laid his shotgun about five feet away from his head. She hung up her underwear on the barbed wire fence. They were deep into the act when he heard an animal snort. He thought it was his mule. That did not stop them. But when he heard a man cough, it got his attention. His friend was watching him and his wife in the act of adultery. Immediately, the party was over. The woman ran off and left her underwear hanging on the fence. When she ran, the friend turned his mule around and rode off.

Daddy shared that he was paranoid and decided that he had better kill his friend. Because this was his worldview had he run upon another man having sex with his wife. So, Daddy was carrying a gun in case their paths crossed. Daddy reported that one day he ran into his friend at the neighborhood store. He was shocked when the friend spoke to him as if nothing had happened. Daddy said that his friend told him, "Mr. Buster, I hear that you are carrying a gun to kill me." Daddy told his friend, "Well, I figured that had I caught you with my wife, I would have killed you so I only saw it fitting that you would feel the same way. I was going to kill you before you killed me." According to Daddy, his friend explained that he understood that Daddy was lonely sometimes and that was why he had invited him to have dinner with him and his wife from time to time. It seems to me now, that the friend and his wife were involved in some kinky stuff and that Daddy was just a target and did not know it. In hindsight, since I knew the friend and saw how obese he was, he was probably using Daddy as a surrogate to help him keep his wife. I doubted that his friend could satisfy his wife sexually because of his obesity and that he did not want to lose her because she was such a good cook.

I was an old woman before I was able to read a book by a Christian author, who explained what happens when a person engages in the sexual act. From reading the book, I learned that the physical, the spirit and soul become intertwined and has a lasting effect. This union forms soul ties, whether healthy or unhealthy. Now, I finally understand the reason that sex outside of marriage is immoral: It upsets God's order and standard for reproduction in humanity. This is the one area that I struggle with and must repent from repeatedly. Lust of the flesh, lust of the eye and pride of life are intermingled and are all responsible for the fall of many. I am not saying that sex is the only area where the lust factor has a stronghold in the lives of men. This lust factor can apply to greed and other ungodly ambitions such as envy, jealousy, powerplay and a desire to please man and his idols. These things, envy, jealousy, and a desire to please others, I have struggled with in life, but find them to be so much easier to overcome than the urge of sex.

One cannot help but wonder why the local church does not have more Bible Study about Lust and how it wrecks the lives of man. It exists everywhere, yet the subject is taboo and is not readily discussed among

Christians. I could also be better educated on how power and sex determine who is dominant in relationship? I have come to know that many women can manipulate the man with sex by refraining from giving him access at all or deciding when he might have access. Having a fear that he would be cut off from sexual activity with the woman, the man becomes subordinate to the woman.

Life has taught me not to covet things that belong to others because we do not always know how they got what they have. Or better yet, how much they had to pay to get what they got. I recall a couple of instances where this revelation came to me. On one occasion, I was in college. I had decided to get a part-time job to help with expenses. One of my sorority sisters gave me a referral to a job. I set up my interview and went to the interview. The logistics getting to the interview were unusual. There were streets, dirt roads and bus changes that I was not familiar with. After getting off the bus, I saw that I had to walk about a block from the bus stop to a trailer. The trailer was the office of the place where the employer was using to sell records. I thought about turning around and going back to the last bus stop. Nevertheless, out of curiosity, I made it to the interview. Once I was there, the first thing the Caucasian employer said to me was, "Get on the cot." Yes, there was a cot there, but I did not make the connection that I was to get on the cot. I was so confused that I just stared at him when he repeated, "Get on the cot." This is when my fight or flight instinct came into play. I turned and dashed out of the trailer and ran back to the bus stop. Once back on campus, I became angry and wanted to curse my big sister out. Then I decided, I would not give her the satisfaction of knowing that I had gone to the interview. If the employer did not tell her that I came I sure did not. I could not help but wonder what her relationship with the man was.

Another incident happened later when I was living in the Atlanta area. My paramour left town to go to a high school class reunion. I was home alone when I received a phone call from my paramour's employer. I remember having told his aunt, our age, that I wanted to go to work and make $50K annually as she was doing. I accepted the invitation to be picked up and driven to the interview by the employer. I did not see this as a red flag. I was not driving yet. I was naïve. I got into the two-toned Javelin automobile that came to pick me up. The driver was black. I was thinking that it was okay to go to the interview because I knew someone affiliated with the company that I was interviewing with. I was driven to the Peachtree Hotel, somewhere in downtown Atlanta. I was escorted into the hotel suite. Noone was in the sitting area. I was then directed to go to a bedroom off to the right. When I stepped into the doorway, I could see three other men standing beside the bed. They all wore white gloves and black suits. I shockingly saw a very large sized person covered under white sheets. There was what appeared to be a huge black male genitalia displayed from underneath a separation in the sheets neatly covering the body from head to toe. This was my cue to flee. It doesn't get any more obvious that I needed to flee the scene. I ran and once on the street, I hailed the first taxi-cab that I saw. The Caucasian driver drove me to my home on the outskirts of the city. When we got to my house, I heard the driver say, $16. I looked in my purse, saw that I only had $9. I threw the $9 to the driver and ran to my apartment there on the first floor. I locked my door and refused to answer when the driver pursued me. He was running around the building banging on doors. I got away.

Again, was I unable to confront the person who had set me up? I often wonder now what she was going to get out of the deal? Was I going to be a sex slave or become a victim of human trafficking? All I could do then was shiver when I thought of what could have happened to be outside of rape. There were five guys there including the one lying on the bed. Today, I thank God about what did not happen to me. I did not tell my paramour when he returned home. I rationalized that it would cause too much chaos and confusion. There was also no telling what that family would have put me through either. I buried the experience in my subconscious. In other words, I did not talk about the experience with anyone. I now wonder if my paramour knew already what had happened that weekend while he was away. I'm just saying...

You Can if You Think You Can

I remember having a first-grade teacher tell me, "Young lady, you have a vast imagination." I believed her and I took advantage of this affirmation. I learned to dream and did not think that there was anything that I could not do. My confidence was high. My confidence soared so highly that others noticed and would cheer me on. This is when I learned that what a teacher says to a student is particularly important in shaping the student's belief in herself and in how the student works harder to impress the teacher to get more 'ego strokes.' This was my cue to let my light shine.

Many of the things that I would do were risky now that I look back. However, Daddy and my older sisters and relatives trusted me to pursue my dreams. My sisters found me to be very entertaining. It was the grace of God that most of my dreams were moral and aspiring. I had escaped repercussions for the few immoral acts that I performed so far. I was a risk taker. Afterall, I had seen others perform immoral acts and get away with them.

So, I was off to conquer my world. Afterall, I believed the quotation that "The world is your oyster." This quote first used by William Shakespeare in his play 'The Merry Wives of Windsor' fit me perfectly. I came to realize that one can achieve anything she wants in life if she has faith.

Faith enables one to see like God, to act and think like God. I did not really think that I was God, but I felt that I was not too far off the mark. Afterall, there was much more to experience out in the world than what there was at home. Frankly, even before Daddy's death at my tender age of 12 years, before he became extremely ill, the family finances took a plunge. Daddy was too sick to farm. This meant that the animals would not be fed, and neither would we. Daddy was a subsistence farmer, who fed the family, others in the community and his animals off the land.

At one point, we did not have drinking water. The 300 foot well dried up and we were forced to haul drinking water. Circumstances became difficult, but I never heard Daddy complain.

Daddy's death was also the culmination of a carefree and secure lifestyle for my three sisters and me.

Living on the Farm Without Daddy

The farm, after Daddy died was no longer a farm. There was just a house and a barn. The two mules, Louis, and Kate along with the bulls and cows and hogs were sold by my brother. There were no animals to house in the barn and no one to do the farming. The mules had been used to plow the crops. The mules were also used to pull the wagon, our mode of transportation after Daddy's 1946 Chevrolet was no longer functional.

I remember riding in the car one or two times. I was about 2 years old. I saw that the adults would have to push the car uphill and jump back in to ride downhill or when the road was level. The backseat where my sisters and my friend B. J. would sit was a very hard slab of wood. Our car was brown, unlike the photo below. The car was parked under a tree in front of the house headed downhill. When we girls learned that the car would roll if you knocked it out of gear, some of us would get inside the car to drive it downhill. Luckily, there were no trees or other objects to run into. When Daddy got on to our risky behavior, driving without a license, we got up one morning and the car was no longer there.

A close replica of the 1946 Chevrolet, but Dad's was brown

My sisters would help Daddy chop cotton, pick cotton, milk the cows, feed the hogs and chickens, and do other chores around the farm. But I doubt they had any clue as to how to get the crops growing and the proper time to maintain the crops until harvest time. Livestock needed to be fed and we could not bail hay nor cotton. I witnessed Daddy doing all those things.

I had no clue as to how difficult it was to do them. I remember trying to pick cotton along with my sisters and could never pick over ten pounds. My sisters would pick 80 and sometimes 100 pounds in one session. One time I picked 15-pounds of cotton and was ecstatic! I suppose I should have been learning when I was riding on their sacks as they picked the cotton when I was younger. Nobody pressed the issue that I learn to work in the fields. I just wanted to try because I knew that they were getting paid to pick the cotton by Daddy. If I made $2.00 on a given day picking cotton, I was happy. Bites from cotton worms hurt. Churning milk was one chore that I was trusted to do with supervision. Sometimes I would help feed the hogs and the chickens. That was a messy job. Hogs wallow in mud, are very aggressive and smell like swamp water. Hogs would eat anything that you fed them. Their food was called slop. Slop was any leftovers from the kitchen all mixed up in water. The slop would be poured into troughs in the pig pen and the hogs would eat it. There was a very sour unpleasant smell. When the hog is going to be slaughtered for food, that hog would be separated from the others and fed corn for a month or so. In the Fall of the year, Daddy and my brother would build a stake, kill a hog or two, dip them in a huge cauldron cast iron pot in boiling hot water to scrap the hair off. Daddy and my brother would hang the hogs on the tall stakes, cut them from the neck down the front and let the inner parts fall into a wash tub. Every part of the hog was edible, including the brains. The females were not allowed to eat mountain oysters, but the men would have the women in the kitchen frying them as they worked on butchering the hogs. Sometimes, there was a cow slaughtered in the same manner. The hams were cured with borax, smoke flavor and salt and put into a smoke house. A cured ham would now cost about $60.

I learned later that the lard from the pig's skin that I used on my customers' hair worked better than most other hair pressing oils that the customers would bring to style their hair with. The Hair Rep, Queen Bergamot, Royal Crown, and other brands only had a better smell than the lard that I used. I did not have to buy anything because we got the lard from the hogs that Daddy killed once a year to feed the family. The lard was the grease that came off the cracklings. Cracklings are the skins of the hogs, which were cooked in large Cauldron Pots after Daddy had built large fires under them.

I made my money pressing and curling hair for all the black women in the community. I learned to style hair with Mama's implements (a straightening comb and marcel iron) that she left behind. I became exceptionally good at what I was doing. I was in business full-time at age 7. I styled hair all day Saturdays.

I learned to style hair by combing my dolls' hair and by transforming a corn shuck into a doll and curling and braiding the hair-like shuck after combing it before it became dry and straw-like before I was four years old. It was very entertaining for me. I became exceptionally good at what I was doing. My pressing and curling talent became so good that I would finger wave the hair once I had curled the client's hair. A style would last two weeks or longer. Most of the women's hair was still set when they came back for a fresh style two weeks later even in the summertime in Mississippi. That was saying massive things about my talent. I also did not know that you had to have a license to style hair. I learned years later that illegally engaging in the profession of cosmetology without a license could cause me to be fined and or incarcerated. So, when the number one black hairstylist in Pickens sent me word that she was going to report me to the State Board of Cosmetology because I had taken all her customers, I had no clue as to what she was saying. By the time I found out what she was saying, I was off to college. The extra money helped me even when I began attending college.

I was lucky in my 'bootleg' practice that I did not have to shampoo, condition or wet set my clients' hair. The clients would come already shampooed and dry. All I had to do was press the hair, curl it and sometimes finger wave the hair. I probably would have lost my passion for the profession had I known then all that being a beautician entail.

It took years later for me to find out the ramifications of what I was doing when I enrolled in Ultissima Beauty College in St. Louis, Missouri in 1987. In beauty college, I learned that sanitation is extremely important in the profession of cosmetology. Back then, the cost to enroll in beauty school was also expensive, $8,000. I was blessed to get a grant to offset the expenses. 1220 course hours were needed to get the certificate and I had to go to Jefferson City, Missouri to do the practical and the written examinations for licensure. I got the license for hairdressing and manicuring.

My second oldest sister (she had a haircut here).

The photo is of one of my most challenging clients, my sister, the second oldest of the four of us. She had the kind of hair that was not African American, not Caucasian, not Native American, just challenging enough to make the hairdresser pull her own hair out. It was about 20 inches long back then. She always wanted it pressed, curled then fingerwaved.

I did not learn until 30 years later in Beauty School that what I was doing was hard pressing the hair. So, I suppose I could be called a young Madame C.J. Walker and at the time and I did not even know of her then. The beauty school I attended did not even teach the art of pressing and curling hair with a marcel iron. I was the only student in the school who knew how to work with the marcel iron. It is unfortunate that we sometimes do not know our financial worth. Even the salons would charge a client more money to get the press and curl or they would tell the client that did not provide that service. In school, I was to learn to permanent wave, relax, shampoo, set and condition hair. Haircoloring and cutting were not as highly emphasized. I would learn more about Haircoloring and cutting later during work as a licensed professional.

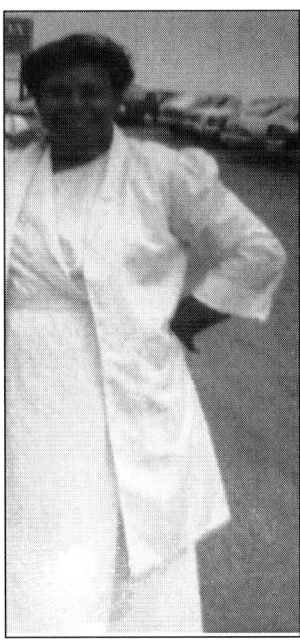

Photo of me getting ready for the exam in Jefferson City, MO

You Do not Skip Any Stages in Development

If my parents were married and home together, I would say that I was truly a child. Even, then I had an air of independence, playing alone when I had three older sisters to play with. I ostracized them because Mama would whip everybody if one of us did something wrong. She said that she whipped everybody because she wanted to make sure that she got the right culprit. I aspired to be as grownup as my sisters, but Mama and the other Church Sisters thought otherwise. I remember once that Easter was coming up and all my sisters had to learn Easter Speeches. I was not given a speech because of my age (2). When the program was taking place, I vividly recall walking to the front of the church making a speech. I am sure that it did not rhyme, but it was loud, and it was about Jesus. The audience was in awe because of my age and clapped loudly.

Not long after, I lost this dogged determination to compete with my sisters. I was going to need them because Mama decided that she no longer wanted to be married to Daddy, leaving him with 4 girls from age 8 to age 3. One morning Daddy thought that he could run a quick errand in his fields before I awakened and come home and cook my breakfast before I was out of bed. He had a nice fire in the fireplace to keep me warm. I awakened and saw that he was not home. I got out of bed and became creative. I had always wanted to have my hair straightened with the pressing comb like Mama did my sisters' hair. She never would do mine. Although I did not have access to a pressing comb, I figured that a fork would do just as well. I did not realize that Mama did not get the pressing comb red hot. So, I got the fork red hot and began to press my hair. Now my hair is in flames! I must stop the flames! Luckily, there was a window with a curtain not far away from the fireplace. I used the curtain to snuff out the flames. Now the curtain was in flames! The window was very tall, almost reaching the ceiling. I jumped and pulled to snatch the burning part of the curtain from the window and luckily the flames stopped. There was smoke and a strong stench. When Daddy came home, he sniffed, but did not mention nor inquire of me about the fire. There was no doubt that he was aware that there had been a fire. The room stank from the burned curtains and from my scorched hair. Two days later Daddy announced that I was going to live with my brother and his wife and that they had a little girl my age. This little girl, a couple of months older than me was my niece. We hit it off right away. My other three sisters were going to live with an older married sister right up the hill from my brother's house. Daddy was cunning and of course, we were not his first set of children. I had siblings by Daddy who were the same age as Mama or just a couple of years younger. And because Daddy had given his first set of children their inheritance before-hand when they got married, he saw it fitting that they pitch in and help with the four of us by Mama after she left home.

Daddy was a subsistence farmer. He never worked for anyone else. Therefore, he needed to figure out how to produce the money to get his retirement income started. Back then, I was almost three years old. My parents conceived me when Daddy was 60 years old. Daddy would be able to retire at age 65. Obviously, Daddy was working while we were away as he was able to pay the $900 to get his retirement check started. We were able to go back home to live with him two years later.

I still was unable to begin school when I turned 5 years old because I did not become 5 years old at the beginning of the year. I was born in February. My niece became 5 years old in December the year before. She was able to enroll in school. I went home with my sisters, who were all in school.

Daddy and I became buddies. He was my sole babysitter for a year. Daddy took me everywhere he went. I learned a lot hanging out with him and he seemed not to be bothered by having me tag along. Daddy was probably grateful that I could walk and get around on my own. Rumors were out that Daddy was a mean man. To this day, I hear other relatives describe Daddy as such. I saw firsthand what Daddy was capable of when he punished a boy that he kept for a year or two for one of the single-parent neighbors, who had to go to the hospital and stay with her son in the burn unit. He whipped the 13-year-old boy with a leather whip. The scene was horrifying. However, the boy was a repeat offender of drinking molasses by the gallon. The whipping did not draw blood. But the boy screamed loudly. I learned later in life that the whipping did not kill him; but the molasses contributed to his death when he was an older man. I learned to stay in the safety zone with Daddy based on observation.

I still try to figure out how Mama would constantly repeat and threaten to bring us children into obedience when Daddy only had to clear his throat once and all of us kids would fall into submission. Many years later, I learned that the man is 'the king of the jungle' and when the lion roars, the earth trembles.

It Takes a Village to Raise a Child

My sisters and I were forced to grow up faster that other kids as Mama was absent and the oldest ones had to take on the adult role of a mother in the home. We were self-governed. It was not long before we felt that we did not need a mother. The oldest of the four of us had been well taught by Mama before she left home and by an older sister where the other three of my sisters lived for the two years that I was away from home. I identified the oldest of the four of us as Mama because she took care of me (grooming, taught me the facts of life and everything else regarding survival based on her knowledge and wisdom at the age of 10).

The oldest of the four of us was adept at money management and shopping for girls, as Daddy gave her the reins. I recall one Easter, she was given money to buy our Easter clothes, something children are not privy to these days. She had us looking good. She also purchased each of us a petticoat. The petticoats would make the dress stand out from the waist to the hemline. The girl looked very feminine. We all looked like ballerinas all dressed up to go to church without Daddy. As we were leaving the house, Daddy asked us where we were going with those petticoats on. For good reason, he demanded, and we had to take off our petticoats before we left home. The oldest had bought herself a 300-yard, The second oldest, a 250-yard, the next oldest, a 100-yard and me a 25-yard petticoat. We loved our petticoats. What I did not like was that the petticoat would deflate as the day wore on. The petticoat would then have to be starched with flour starch, which dried in the petticoat and would fall out as the girl walked. The starch would stick to the fishnet fabric the petticoat was made of and make it stand out again. The starched garment would last for a day or so. Like all fashion, the petticoat soon was out of style.

Below is a photo of the oldest of the four of us, my sister who took over the family role as mother when she was a mere 8 years old. She was older here, about 12 or 13 years old. She has been the boss ever since.

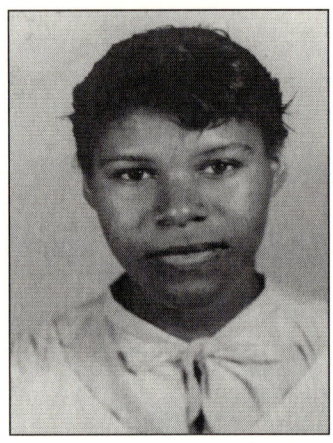

It was a bit unsettling and sad that Daddy was forced to raise 4 girls alone ranging in ages from 8 to 3. Many people in the community were not sorry for him. They felt that daddy deserved what he got. As I had mentioned earlier, Daddy had a reputation for being intimidating and mean tempered. I felt sorry for daddy and for myself. And it took me years to get over the bitterness of Mama leaving us. Forgiving Mama was really a necessary thing for me to do as I could see that she had some mental issues going on. That was a pattern of having babies, taking them home to her parents or giving them away to others. It took years, before I was able to do it and I have a sense of peace and wellbeing as a result. It took my granddaddy these comments to me about how he had spoiled Mama. He called her 'Froggy.'

My sisters and I could be called little women well before our time. We were not children long. We did the things we wanted to do and what we needed to do to survive. We were resilient. Somehow, despite this resilience, Daddy thought that we needed a mother. But it was too far into the game for us to see it that way. I can only imagine that he wanted a woman to come and clean house because we were not good with that job. When Daddy tried to bring women to meet us and introduced them as a candidate for our mother, we would ask him, "Where is she going to live?" He got the message as it would be a repeat experience of when his first set of kids ran his second wife away. That marriage ended in a nasty divorce. The divorce became the 'talk of the town' as they say. Although I was not born yet, the story still had life when I was able to discern that adults had disagreements. It would be not much later that I would learn that older people did evil deeds as well.

I doubt that there were social workers in rural Mississippi during that time (especially accessible to black families) unless the family was a part of the welfare system. It seemed to be understood that Daddy was financially capable of taking care of us. The Social Workers were kept at bay.

If it takes a village to raise a child, the village disappeared as soon as Mama left the home. My adult sister, who was soon to pass away when I was about five years old, visited rarely. And unfortunately, my sister My older sister died about the time I was 5 years old. I remember being unable to sleep as I visualized the casket being beside the bed where I was sleeping. It was not until Daddy's death when I was 12 years old that I began to overcome my fear of dead people. Of course, he was Daddy. We were very closely knit, and I knew that he would not harm me.

No one else came by to visit unless they needed Daddy to give them something or have him blacksmith their plow points and put shoes on their mules.

I had nightmares about my sister's death and could not sleep before she was buried. I would envision the casket being beside the bed where I slept with one of my other sisters. This time, I was not sleeping in the middle as I did with Mama and Daddy. There was only one other sister in bed beside me. The casket was right there beside the bed where I was. I got no sleep that night. When my grownup sisters from Cleveland, Ohio visited for the funeral, I was distracted and was able to take my mind off the deceased. I was finally able to sleep.

My great fear of dead bodies came from times when Mama would scream and cry at funerals so much that other women there would have to take me away from her to comfort me as I was crying because she was crying. Mama seemed to forget that I was afraid of any person who was not in my immediate family. The women all wore black and many of them wore Estee Lauder Youth Dew cologne. From that day on, I disliked Youth Dew Cologne. The fragrance was very potent and had it not been for the reminder of funerals, I would have appreciated it more when my boy-friends' mothers would gift it to me. I accepted the gifts graciously. I wore the fragrance with funerals in the back of my head. Once the fragrance got into your clothes you could not wash it out.

I did not get rid of my fear of dead people until Daddy died at home. There was something about the fact that he was Daddy, and I was not afraid of him.

Later in life, I ran into dead bodies in the streets and on one occasion in a bathroom. I was not so frightened by them. I suppose Daddy cured me. So, when I had hands-on dealing with a dead body when my sister, next to me died and I, being a beautician, was appointed to do her hair I was not afraid. I went to the funeral home and did what I needed to do as she laid there on the cooling board. However, I was not impressed with the funeral home staffs trying to spook me by not putting brakes on the cooling board. So, when I began to work, the cooling board cart started rolling slowly across the floor. The staffs were watching from behind the curtain and pretended not to know that the brake was off. They corrected the problem immediately. Unfortunately, I had a dream that the hairstyle had messed up and did not survive the body's lying-in state overnight at the church.

I recall that Daddy always tried to prepare us for the unforeseen. He once said that when he died, he would not scare us; he would just pull the covers up and perhaps pull our toes. He had a cunning sense of humor. I had forgotten this when I got a chance to revisit it when I was about 34 years old living in Los Angeles, California. I left work early, decided to take a nap and was awakened by my bed shaking. I thought the shaking was from Daddy. At once I telephoned my sister back in Chicago, Illinois to tell her that my Daddy had visited me. Later that evening while watching the news, I learned that a small town about 80 miles away was leveled by an earthquake. I believe the town was named Normal, California. I was from the Midwest and had not experienced tremors and earthquakes to that degree. I do remember seeing the picture frames on my mother in law's walls shift one day earlier. However, I assumed that I had an illusion as the picture frames shifted back into place immediately.

I am grateful that I was able to live in Los Angeles two years and move away without experiencing 'the big one' everyone was always talking about. I noticed that wall hangings and pictures would shift from time to time, but never the big one. I also had witnessed the buckling pavement on a couple of the streets near East Los Angeles.

I was not sociable at all while Mama was living at home. I would run under the house when visitors came by to see Mama. Mama did not come to get me because she knew that I would be coming out to eat after her company left. What she did not know is that I had learned to steal pint jars of canned tomatoes, preserved peaches and pears. I would eat as much as I could and hide the remainder until I wanted more under the house. Mama knew I was stealing tomatoes when I would have a case of Nettle Rash. Although the rash did not last very long, it was excruciating. I would itch all over my body, including in the palms of my hands and the soles of my feet. I was then running to Mama to get help for the itching. Although she probably knew what I had done, she did not punish me.

Fear is a State of Mind

I believe that if someone does not give you a reason to fear, you will not fear. I think that it is remarkably interesting that I did not fear animals and wildlife that could harm me; but I feared strangers and airplanes, most of which were crop dusters. The appearance of an airplane was a guarantee that I would be returning home, that is after pulling myself up from the ground. I would fall prostate until the airplane left the area. I would then run as fast as I could to get home.

Even before Mama left home and far into my youthful years, I was a loner and a wanderer. I could wander away from home and Mama or family members would not have a clue as to where I was and what I was doing. I felt very secure wandering in the woods and around our 50 plus acre property.

I had a great imagination and curiosity which would propel me to wander farther and farther away from home. Sometimes I would find myself wandering on the bordering properties of my neighbors. Most of those properties had no homesteads or the houses on the properties would be vacant. One of the properties was interesting to me because the empty house had a piano in it on the first floor. I would go to the house and do my version of playing the piano. There were two to three cisterns around the house. Thankfully, they did not attract me enough to fool around and get myself drowned in one of them. One day when I was in the house, I could hear someone walking upstairs. When I learned that I was not alone, I ran out of the house. I knew I was out of my territory when I went to the house. The property was well-kept, despite its vacancy. Rumor had it that the property belonged to a rich white man and that he had left the property to go to Hollywood and play the role of 'The Lone Ranger'. Research on the rumor did not confirm the rumor, but who knows. Guy Mansell could have had a pen name in Hollywood.

Another of my trespassing wanderings was an adjacent property belonging to one of Daddy's friendly neighbors. I was fascinated by the pond there which was surrounded by Catskill plants. I would stand on the bank and imagine Moses flowing downstream in the waterproof crib just as it was described in the Bible. Again, I was out of earshot of anyone who could rescue me had I needed rescue. I was at least one-half mile away from home. Luckily, I did not have a scare over there. The earth was red over there on that hill. It was just beautiful. I suspect that if Daddy used to own 366 acres of land, that this property would have been part of what he sold. I cannot imagine why he would sell this property. I loved it.

Sometimes this property owner would come and work on the land. I could not readily see what kind of farming he was doing. I do not recall seeing any mules or any other animals on the land. But the land was rather neat. and cared for.

This landowner would chat with Daddy when we went over there together. He was the only white man I saw Daddy interact with in a friendly manner. He offered Daddy and me a drink from his five-gallon lemonade keg. The lemonade was delicious.

When Daddy would take me to the cotton gin in Goodman and then take me to the general store, where he was not seemingly nice to the store owners who were white. I was later to learn that these store owners were Jews, and that Daddy was kin to them. When the store owner would tell my daddy the price of whatever he had bought, that it always gave them a hard time and did not want to pay taxes. One of my nephews reminded me how that if the store owner told Daddy a different price than what daddy had figured or then what he had told that in the cost of the item was, that it would want to know what the difference was. Daddy would call the store owner by his first name saying, "Taxes? Allen, you know I don't pay no damn taxes. " Daddy would then storm out of the store pulling me by the hand. Daddy only paid the principle. This was very abnormal behavior for a black man to have in Mississippi. And I did not see Daddy acting this way with any other white people in Mississippi. There certainly was some kind of relationship there that was cordial, having understanding. These were the only two stores that Daddy frequented there in Goodman.

I was about four years old and could not swim. It was a great hobby of mine to go to the pond, downhill from our house and look for crawdads and frogs. Sometimes I would find a Turpan and torture him. One day I was playing on the muddy side of the pond. There was a large amount of grass there and somehow, I ended up falling into the pond. I had a struggle getting out before drowning. I thought that the grass would help me pull myself out, but it kept becoming uprooted and I would go back under the water. I learned that the pond was deeper on that end than the end where my sisters and I would go skinny dipping with our friends.

When I finally dragged myself out of the pond, I went back to the house all muddy and wet. Daddy, wise and cunning, just glanced at me and kept walking. The next day, he killed and brought the largest cotton mouthed moccasin into the back yard and laid him there dead for the chickens and the dogs to eat I figured.

The snake was larger in circumference than my waist. These days when I think on this, I have to wonder if Daddy was feeding the snake. Obviously, he knew the snake, a cotton-mouthed moccasin, was living in the pond there by the willow tree.

I do not remember hearing Daddy tell us not to do anything often. He would just correct the situation to keep us alive when there was a threat. There were many of those times. Some of the memories are vividly still with me.

Daddy was a blacksmith and a farmer. His customers would bring their plow points to him to sharpen and their horses and mules to get shoed. The customers would get comfortable while waiting to get their work done. They would take off their shoes. We girls called them 'clod knockers.' The customers would cut out the shoes to vent in the summertime. June, July and August are very hot months in Mississippi.

My sisters would go to the pond and find crayfish and put them in the shoes. When the men would put their shoes on, the crayfish would pinch their toes. The men would not tell Daddy what my sisters had done. So, the girls went unpunished for that sin. We thought that was very funny.

Rumor had it that people were afraid of Daddy. I do know that when he raised his voice, everybody trembled. I wonder if that is how he earned the nickname 'Buster'. Mama and many of the people in the community called him 'Mister Buster'. His older children called him, 'Papa'. My sisters and I called him, 'Daddy'. For the sake of brevity and relevance, I will be calling him 'Daddy' for the rest of this writing.

Daddy also had a sense of humor. Daddy would sometimes tell me tales of funny things that happened over the years when he was raising his first set of his children, who were approximately the same age as Mama.

Daddy told me a tale of two brothers who had a blood curling fight over biscuits during lunch time at school. One brother was going to kill his brother over a biscuit.

Another funny story Daddy told me was about two brothers who had a fight over a horse. The brothers thought that everything should be divided equally when the father died. They had this horse and could not figure out how to divide it. So, they decided to cut the horse into two equal parts.

I continued to wander as I grew older, well into my preteens. I must wonder how I would end up being alone many times, not knowing where my other siblings were.

I enjoyed hanging out down by our pond. In the springtime, very tall straw-like grass would grow up between the pond and the house. One day I was playing by the pond and was standing by the tall grass when an awfully long snake came up from the swamp that was bordering our property and a neighbor's property. The snake was traveling amazingly fast. His tail was parting the grass and making a swishing sound. The snake was right upon me before I could run or do anything. Somewhere along the way, I had learned that snakes could bite and constrict people and kill them.

This snake's head was at least four feet off the ground. When he passed me, I had to look up at him. Acting as if he did not see me, the snake went up to the forest area and climbed a tree so tall that I had to lean back to see the top of the tree. The snake's head was at the top of the tree and his tail was still on the ground.

I was in awe. I took a mental note of this. We did have monsters living around us.

I learned early on that we had ghosts living around us as well. I had a habit of playing out back in the yard with the chickens, cats, and dogs while Mama prepared and cooked breakfast for me. We always had homemade biscuits, meat, gravy, and eggs for breakfast. In the spring and summertime, we would also have tomato gravy. We were never hungry, and Daddy grew all the food that we ate. His garden was at least one acre in size. The only thing that he had to buy from a grocery store was meal, flour, and sugar.

As I played in the backyard right off the kitchen where Mama was cooking breakfast with the back door open, I looked up toward the barn and noticed a very nicely dressed man walking toward our house. He was wearing a black suit, a very white shirt, had a lantern in his left hand, but he had no head. The other odd thing about this handsomely dressed man is that he was able to walk through the two-stranded barbed wire fence right near the house where I was playing. I noticed that the dogs started barking and the chickens went wild and panicked, running away. I ran to the kitchen to Mama. I do not recall telling her what I had seen.

Later in life I learned that Mama was already aware of the ghosts, who she said were Daddy's older children and relatives who had passed away years ago. I figured that the ghost I saw was Daddy's oldest son, Bigum, who was killed working at a sawmill.

There was a black and white portrait of Bigum and his fiancé at our house. After his death, the fiancé' married another man and I was able to meet her and go to school with her children. The photo showed a very handsome couple. Rumor had it that he was the talk of the town, among the women because he was so handsome. The photo was taller than I was at the time, and it was framed in a mahogany brown oval shaped mahogany frame. The glass was dome-shaped to fit the frame. Now that I think of it, the portrait was exceptionally fine and would cost a large amount of money today.

One thing about the portrait of him that caught my attention was that he had extremely long arms. The long arms were one of the noticeable features that caused me to know that the ghost was him. Once the ghost stepped through the fence and not over the fence, he disappeared.

I did not see any ghosts after that incident, but later when I was older, I heard one speak. It was a female. On another occasion when I was about 12 years old, my sister heard a female speak through our radio, which was not operative because the battery was dead. These incidents involved the same ghost manifesting herself. This ghost manifested around the time of Daddy's final illness. She was always looking for 'Papa.' This is the name Daddy's older children called him.

When Daddy first got sick, the family was sitting around the table that we had put in the living room eating bologna and crackers. Our neighbor, w was visiting. The female ghost knocked on the door and asked, "Is Papa home?" The ghost was impatient. As nobody was expecting any visitors around eight or nine PM, nobody moved. We all just sat there and looked from one to the other in a puzzled manner. The ghost asked again louder, "Is Papa home?" Our neighbor, being the only other male present, was sitting nearest the door. Daddy asked him to answer the door. When he answered the door, nobody was out there. We did not have a porch light and there was no streetlight as there was no street. Our visiting neighbor said, "I looked, I didn't see nobody, and I'm gone!" He slammed the door and ran home. Daddy sat there looking 'all knowing' but did not say a word. The next day, Daddy was hospitalized.

The last time she visited and spoke loudly to my sister, who was hiding her school supplies under the radio battery. Back in the early 1960's, the radio battery was the size of a shoe box. The battery was a good hiding place for a ream of paper. After being scolded by Daddy to give me paper after I had explained that I had used all of mine, my sister was shocked when she went to the radio to get paper for me that she had hid under the radio that was setting on top of the dead battery. The battery had died several months earlier. I had no problem getting the paper when my sister heard the voice asking through the radio, "Is Papa home?" My sister hurriedly brought me the paper. Had it been another situation, we would have been fighting about my asking for more paper. Funny that the woman on the radio would ask through the radio setting atop a dead battery.

Daddy was bedridden and would not have been anywhere but home or in the hospital. Daddy died in the next couple of days. This was the last time that I experienced ghosts on the property. We continued to live there after Daddy's death. This was home and we had nowhere else to go. We did not have rent or other bills. We owned the house and the land free and clear. Therefore, we were able to live on the small Social Security Check that we received.

Mama and I lived there after my older siblings had moved on until the first half of my senior year of high school. This was our home, but it was no longer a farm.

Although there were no telephones and other modern-day amenities available to most of the families in the community, there was a 'grapevine,' and it served its purpose. Now that I think back, our neighbor's son, who had dropped out of school and was severely burned. The third-degree burns had made him totally disabled. He already had been suspended permanently from school because he attacked a teacher. He spent his time acting as the 'pony express.' He would wander, snoop around and was knowledgeable about many things before others would even conceive of knowing. He would also hang out in the bushes and spy on others. He never got caught. He had a wealth of first-hand knowledge, which oftentimes was helpful to the survival of the residents of the community.

I have often pondered on what time or age a person is when they begin to consider that their purpose is other than they are the result of their parents' lust. Of course, I never spent a large amount of time on the thought before I had the revelation that a change in basic assumptions had to take place in my life. Again, this revelation only happened after I learned that I had exhausted all my options to fail with a logical explanation. If you consider yourself intelligent, you must be able to stand under your truth, even if your truth is not "THE TRUTH. You must think that your truth is valid, rational, morally, and politically correct. When standing under your truth, you must think that "your truth" is embraced by the world and that it is acceptable, but not necessarily moral. Frighteningly so, the World will embrace your truth as long as your truth is not "The Truth". The paradigm shift, by revelation had to convey to me that I must try "The Truth" because everything else that I had tried had ended in failure. I will not be too hard on myself because I did not know that I was operating out of ignorance, that I was picking inadequate role models, being self-centered, straddling the fence by adopting some of the principles of "The Truth" and others of the "world's truth". I would then test my theories and find failure in my testing. The theories were oftentimes based on my effort to survive. At those times when I believed that my recipe for survival was "The Truth", I really did not realize that I was exercising a fatal degree of ignorance. This is a good place to say, "If I knew then, what I know now, I would have done many things differently." It would be many other experiences and years before I was given the revelation that I needed to try "The Truth" because of all truths, it would be sustained by God's love and grace.

The Political Landscape Divides the Haves and the Have-not's

Even though, Daddy had land and had never been a slave, he was forced to struggle and fight against 'Jim Crow Law'. We girls were sheltered from dealing with 'Jim Crow Law' because we rarely ventured outside our habitat. I have learned over the years from reading accounts of family history, that Daddy was of Jewish and Native American Descent. Daddy's father's father was a Jew. Daddy's mother was Native American. I also came to know that Daddy's Paternal Grandfather had his father by a woman of another race, because Daddy's father was listed in the records as being biracial person. Daddy had a dark complexion, and his hair was not straight and wavy like his brother Adam's was. I have heard it said and very much assumed that the older folks did not talk about the negative side of the past. I often wondered how my maternal grandparents got married as my maternal grandfather looked like a white man and my maternal grandmother looked like she was from Africa. Her complexion was very dark. Now that I recall, my maternal side of the family did not talk about the past, but Daddy talked a plenty.

I learned that the Caucasian neighbor who owned the adjoining property on the right hated black people and that he and his friends had given Daddy a hard time simply because they did not want him to own all that land that he had. I learned that they wanted him to sell the land to him and his friends (obviously the Ku Klux Klan). This kind of activity caused

Daddy to have to put up signs around the borders of his property: 'Posted Keep Out'. I also learned later in life, that Daddy was so traumatized by the illegal activities of the Ku Klux Klan, that he would sit on the front porch with his double-barreled shotgun on his lap. Oftentimes, he would fall asleep with the gun on his lap. I can only imagine that the hatred had mostly to do with the color of Daddy's skin. I saw that the other Caucasian people around there, many of whom were Jews, did not have problems with the Ku Klux Klan. I also saw that their properties were not as large as Daddy's. I learned from reading deeds left around the house that at one time, Daddy owned 366 Acres of land and that he had sold some of the land to some of the friendly Caucasians and gave his first set of children about 40 Acres each when they married, left home in good standing with Daddy and decided to live on the land that he gave them. I also came to know that some of the older children only got 30 Acres and others got 20 Acres if they moved away to Cleveland, Ohio. The flourishing automotive industry in Cleveland beaconed one of the boys to take his wife and five children to Cleveland, Ohio after he had served time in the army. This son had built a house on his 30 Acres. He saw a more prosperous future working in the factory than with farming.

Daddy kept 50 Acres for himself, farmed and fed his new wife, Mama and the four girls that he had by her. He was able to manage the 50 Acres left and kept his farm animals. Daddy used the house that my older brother left to lease out to sharecroppers, who were usually connected to the family by marriage or kinship. None of the families stayed exceptionally long. I recall four families living there over two years if you counted my brother and his family. One of the other families was a sharecropper. Another was my maternal grandparents.

Daddy soon learned that sharecropping was not profitable for him as neither of his sharecropper families were genuinely wanting to farm. Somehow, he had to be convinced by the fact that at the end of the year the families would owe him more than he had given them to farm. Neither family had a mule or farm equipment. Daddy needed his mules, Louis, and Kate, to work his crops and for transportation. By the time he had married Mama and the four of us girls, his 1946 Chevrolet had stopped working.

Daddy had learned to do more with less. There was evidence that he had more money and wealth before his third marriage. There was evidence around the homestead that economics were better in times past. There was an automobile, which was losing its steam. I was able to ride in it twice. I recalled sitting on the back seat with my friend, Bettie Jean or with one of my sisters. The adults would have to get out of the car and push it uphill, jump back in and ride downhill or when the road became level again. It was not long before the Chevrolet was parked under a tree down the hill in front of the house. We girls, who could be dubbed tomboys, would get in the car, and push it downhill. It was not long before Daddy got rid of the car. Luckily, there were no other trees or roadblocks in the way to wreck the car and hurt us. Evidence around the homestead also showed me that the first set of kids had a good education. They attended private schools, some as far away as Jackson, which was far away from Goodman. The students would have to live in a dormitory or in a boarding home. Back then, a student would graduate upon completion of the eighth grade. The older kids were more affluent. They had an organ with a pedal, a phonogram, which played records that were about a fourth of an inch thick and other artifacts were on the property, which were not necessities for living, but for creature comfort and entertainment.

People visited from different communities often to be blessed by Daddy, usually with food. Back then, 'you did not let your right hand know what your left hand was doing'. I recall that Daddy allowed a family of three to live with us for two years when the mother was forced to go and live at the hospital with one of the children, who was severely burned. The mother had tried to smother flames with water when her son's night clothes caught fire when he was making a fire for the family to warm by when they awakened for the day. She had no idea of what 'drop and roll' meant. The child had permanent scars. The family was extremely poor. The mother expressed signs of mental disorder. She had an exceptionally good heart and came to be one of the most influential persons in our lives when Mama left home.

Mama worked around the home. But she worked extremely hard, all the time. She was an excellent cook and homemaker. Mama did not allow kids to take naps during the daytime. She made her beds early in the day. They were not to be disturbed until nighttime. She liked to entertain, and Daddy made sure that she had what she needed to cook to do so. People were always coming to eat and going. I would be jealous when others came by because I wanted Mama's attention all the time. I felt that Daddy's children from Cleveland were demanding too much of her attention when they would come down to visit for two weeks three families at a time in the summertime. Most of them lived at our house. I was very jealous. One of Mama's other daughters also was there. It seemed to me that Mama was tied to the kitchen stove for two weeks. She did not seem to ever get tired.

Mama's oldest daughter from another union, came to live with us. She had left her husband and was pregnant with her oldest daughter. She was unbelievably beautiful. It was not long before she was courting Daddy's nephew who had lost his first wife to death. The nephew soon got the word that my sister was living there with us, and he would visit with his younger brother. They would both be dressed in US Army Uniforms. I am not sure that either of them was still in the military at that time. The uniforms were impressive to Mama. She would get extremely excited when she saw them coming and would begin to fuss and dance around singing, "Here Comes the Preacher Man." She made me curious. Even at the age of 2 and a half years old, I could sense that there was something wrong with that kind of behavior. I never wanted to share Mama. It was not long before my sister had her baby and got married to Daddy's nephew and moved away. I saw the birth of the baby to an extent. I was told to go outside in the back yard and watch the stork fly over with the baby in a blanket. I went outside and looking up, I could picture a stork flying overhead with a baby in its beak a cloth the size of a diaper. The weather was stormy. The baby was a beautiful little girl. Daddy's nephew already had four children. So, he and my sister became a blended family. They remained married until his death.

When my sister moved away, Mama became depressed and began to say, "I want to have some pleasures of my life." I am not sure what she meant by that. I cannot say that Daddy was impotent or something of that nature. I slept with them, and I do not recall their moving me from between them in bed. But who knows? I guess none of us will ever get to know the answer to that because none of us had the nerve to ask her, despite our curiosity. One thing that we know for sure is that she did not raise any of her nine children and that the one of us that she spent more time with was my brother whose father was a military man. She received financial help from him. Mama had stayed with the military man, her next oldest daughter and her son birthed by the military man. She was keeping her daughter because there was nobody to raise her that Mama trusted. Mama's parents already had taken custody of her oldest daughter, her oldest son, and another child of one of my uncles. The parents had more kids than they could handle already. Her second son and her second daughter had gone to live with their paternal grandparents. However, there was something about the second daughter that caused Mama to take her away from the paternal grandparents and try to raise her along with her third son, whose father was the military man.

Mama, her second daughter & her third son

Mama was successful raising her second daughter for a while, but shortly after there was a breakup with the military man. Mama began to give the second daughter to family members out of state. The second daughter was about sixteen years old before I came to know her. She was 14 years old when I was born. She built rapport with me, and I learned to like her. It was her that I would be visiting in St. Louis summers beginning at age nine.

I can imagine that Mama was of the mindset that I had after I lost my first love. No other man mattered. Mama told me that she was in love with a young man who was a close relative of hers. Neither she or her lover knew they were relatives, and no one had told them that they were because the young man was born out of wedlock and his father was kept a secret. They only learned that they were first cousins when he asked her parents for her hand in marriage. They were so much in love that they wanted to do the right thing, get married before having sex, which was inevitable because of the passion building up between them. There was an unbreakable stronghold. When my maternal grandfather told them that they could not get married because they were first cousins, they were devastated! I was old enough to understand what she meant at the age of fifteen when I found out that this very well could be the root of her inability to love my daddy as I thought she should.

The experience I had when I lost my first love helped me to understand that Mama could never love another after loving him. I had the opportunity to see Mama's heartbeat in person one day when I got home from school. He was absolutely one of the most handsome men I had ever seen in my life. He soon left after I showed up. And I never saw him again.

Trauma Has its Scars

When the breadwinner dies, the foundation of the family is traumatized. When Daddy died, I was severely traumatized. I was shaken in ways that were unimaginable. Firstly, I had to grow up overnight. I was the baby of the family, and everybody treated me as such. I was left to child's play, had no chores, and did not have to make any big decisions about survival. Everything was figured out for me. All I had to do was to show up. Now that Daddy was no longer there, I had to grow up. My sisters were busy trying to figure out their own lives and survival. I was twelve years old. I learned quickly to pay attention to what my older siblings were doing to survive. I learned the good and the bad. Early on in life, I had already exercised my gift of discernment and could smell trouble. Therefore, I bought in to the point where what they were doing was logical. I chose not to buy in when what they were doing was not logical.

My sisters were dating age when Daddy died. Before his death, the girls could only allow boys to come by the house to visit on weekends. Now that Daddy was no longer a barrier to my sisters and their friends seeing boys away from home, Saturday evenings became an outing out on the town. The girls would walk to the nearby town hoping for a ride by someone to pick them up and take them to Pickens, which was about 13 miles from our house. Pickens was not the nearest town to where we lived, but Camden was not as popular for Saturday Night Partying. There were no Honky Tonks in Camden. There were several in Pickens: Walter Body's, Florence Nelson's and another popular one about 300 feet from Florence Nelson's, Big John's. The Honky-Tonk on the main drag was a good one for the teenage crowd. All the others were for the hard-core plantation workers and those who just liked to drink, prostitute and fight. I assessed that if no one was killed on Saturday Night, nobody had any fun. Sadly enough, once the killer went to prison/jail, he did not stay long. The plantation owner had to get the criminal out so that he c work on the plantation. The plantation was in Vaughn, Mississippi, a community nearby Pickens where Jesse James had a train wreck. There is a museum there commemorating Jesse James and his exploits. The only other things notable in Vaughn were the residents and the vast plantation crops. The black residents would venture to Pickens to party on Saturday evenings and nights. If a plantation worker went to jail, the plantation owner would bail them out to ensure that they were working the plantation early Monday Morning.

Party animal, I was not. Being in the pre-college program, Upward Bound which is for indigent, first family members to attend college saved me from the full-fledged party life that I did not care for. If the student competed the program, she would be granted full tuition to attend the college of her choice. She would also receive a stipend weekly for participation. The college would take the students shopping so that they could spend their stipends.

The Upward Bound Program at Tougaloo College in Tougaloo, MS also served as a haven for my protection because although Mama came back to the home shortly before Daddy died, her motive was not good. She had no intention of truly taking care of us girls. She needed an income. She had come to know that while she was out there philandering for nine years, she was not having the pleasures of her life that she dreamed of having. She found out that the man that she was so much in love with had a family and that he was not in love with her. Daddy, a provider, who was always thinking ahead, had convinced Mama on his sick bed that the thing to do was to come home and be there with us girls. She knew that he would not recover from his illness. Daddy could no longer walk on his own. Little did he know that Mama was not going to be home with us often and that she would mostly show up when the check came. Therefore, we girls, all teenagers now, did not think that we needed her. She served one good purpose that we were not aware of at the time. She prevented us from going to foster care. I am certain that this was Daddy's thinking as well.

I was in Upward Bound where I was taught creative writing by the now famous Alice Walker, who was just Alice Walker, a teacher at that time. Had I known that she would become famous, I would have made a greater effort to form a lasting relationship with her. This was another of those, 'if I knew then what I know now' situations. Things would be a great deal better. It was in 1997 that I received a phone call from the now incredibly famous Alice Walker's publishers and was asked to use work that I had written in her creative writing class. She wanted to either put my work at the beginning or at the end of her book. I asked the publisher what the amount of my royalty would be for allowing Alice to use my work. The publisher answered that there would be no royalty for me, even after my telling her that I was struggling to raise a set of twins. The publisher emphasized that Alice wanted to put my work either at the beginning or at the end of the book, which meant that my work would be placed in important places and would gain notoriety. I asked to speak with Alice and was informed that Alice was in Hawaii. I told the publisher that I could not allow my work to be published for free. I did not receive any more phone calls and I did not pursue the matter farther.

It lets me know now, that I was not 'born again' in 1997 or that if I was 'born again', my level of spiritual maturity was low. I was a Christian, but a rather carnal minded one. I realize now that maturation is a process. I had my pride. Losing out on this opportunity was one of my life lessons. Giving of yourself is not always something that you redeem for money. And that exposure through the influence of someone famous could help you reap far more. It has taken a bit of Christian Education and spiritual maturity for me to get the revelation that you do not work to become rich. You are to work to help others and lead them to Truth. Matthew 28:18-20: "All authority has been given to Me in heaven and on earth. Go therefore and make disciples of all the nations, baptizing them in the name of the Father and of the Son and of the Holy Spirit." NKJV

The planning of getting to and back home from the Upward Bound Program was a chore itself. I had friends who would allow me to visit overnight to either connect with transportation to the program or to get back home on the weekend. I would have the bus drop me off in Pickens so that I could meet up with my sisters and their friends for the late night or early morning drive home with different boys who had transportation. I recall that one time I did not have to go to the Upward Bound Program for the weekend. I decided that I did not want to go to Pickens either, despite the fact, that I had a boyfriend in Pickens. I was a nerd, who was always reading various kinds of books. I was reading when other kids were playing and doing other chores. This weekend, I was reading the book Helter-Skelter about the Charles Manson Clan. I decided to stay home alone this Saturday Night. I was okay as long as it was daylight. But at night when it was very dark outside, I began to get really scared. We lived about a mile away from our closest neighbors. The neighbors' girls were gone to Pickens with my sisters and on occasion, my niece would be able to convince her mother to let her spend the night with us and she would be among the crew hitchhiking to Pickens on Saturday evenings. My niece was my age. We had played and lived together, but now as a teenager, she liked to party. I noticed that my niece and I began to drift apart a bit once she started school a year before me. Now, she was maturing faster than me. She wanted to hang out with the older girls. Going to Pickens did not appeal to me.

I did not like the idea that she was able to start school one year earlier than me and she was only two months older than me. We still had a close bond, but it was not as close as it was when we were climbing trees, cutting our hair with her daddy's clippers while her mother was working in the garden and doing other devilish things. She liked to be a tomboy. Now she was liking the night life. This left me alone in the woods hiding under the bed reading a book. Since we did not have electricity, I was forced to take the kerosene lamp under the bed with me. This was a dangerous thing to do. The mattress could have caught fire and the entire house would have burned down. It was 30 years later that I had the experience of witnessing a fire caused by a mattress, which burned an entire building. I was under the bed until four or five o'clock in the morning before I heard my sisters coming home. I had heard the one dog we had left barking. After Daddy died, nobody fed the dogs, so they disappeared as did all the other farm animals we had. My brother and my mother had sold them. I learned that the dog was not barking because my sisters were on their way home. He was barking at something else because the party crew did not come home for another hour. I was very relieved when my sisters finally did come home.

I stayed home alone one Saturday because I was afraid to go to Pickens because I had been threatened by my boyfriend not to come to Pickens again. I had gone to Walter Body's Café after being dropped off from Upward Bound one Saturday Evening. I would arrive in Pickens around 6 PM. My first stop would be Walter Body's to buy myself a Champale, a type of beer. Yes, a youth could buy anything they had the money to buy in Pickens, including other street drugs. I restricted myself to the Champale. Although I was no older than 16 years old, I did not have to show an ID. I would drink my drink there or I would walk and drink on the street as I looked for my sisters at one of the other Honky-Tonks. All of them were walking distance from each other.

On the Saturday before, I had walked into a particular Honky-Tonk and there was my boyfriend sitting across the booth from the tavern owner's daughter. I had unknowingly walked into a drug transaction in progress. I noticed that she handed him a small Domino matchbox after he passed her money rolled up. I suspected that there was where my boyfriend was getting the brown stuff in the match box when he visited me once at my home. This young man was my first love. It really hurt me to hear him yell at me, "I don't want to see you in Pickens again" although I had at once turned to leave the Honky-Tonk when I saw that he and the owner's daughter were the only people there. I could not stand to see him with another female. I was jealous. He was mine. I did not want to confront him there. I would do this later.

I told my sister what my boyfriend said when talk began among my sisters about next Saturday's visit to Pickens. One of my sisters said, "He is not your daddy. He can't keep you out of Pickens." I was afraid to go to

Pickens the next Saturday. I would be home alone because Mama, who had come back home, was rarely there on weekends.

Mama would come, cash our Social Security Check, buy a few groceries and give each of us a $20 allowance for the month. Constant suggestions by my Sister-In-Law and the neighbors that Mama stay home with us girls, did not work. Mama continued her Shenanigans. I could never figure out why she always left home walking to someplace that we were not aware of. None of us had any idea where she was going nor where she was staying, and neither did she tell us anything. She just was not home most of the time. Sometimes she would be gone for a week. We did not ask her anything either. We had gotten used to her being gone as she had been gone away from us for about a decade. We did not think we needed her now, but we did need her for protection.

We would often see Mama walking along the roadways when we were on the school bus. Sometimes the bus driver would pick her up and drop her off someplace along the bus route.

I Thank God that we did not have to pay utilities and rent. Our Social Security Check would not have sustained us. My oldest sister had dropped out of school to get married when she was in the 11th grade. Her boyfriend proposed. Mama encouraged her to marry him telling her that the check would go further if she was out of the house. I now wonder if Mama reported that the child had left the home to the Social Security Administration. I seriously doubt that she did. My sister's husband, one of the neighbor's boys had moved her to Milwaukee and later to Chicago. Mama was supportive of her marriage. Marriage helped her to move on. As time moved on and more of us graduated and left home, those left would not have any more of an allowance. Mama continued to receive a check for me at age eighteen because I was pursuing higher education.

Bright Lights, Big City

I was scared to go to Pickens because I feared what my boyfriend would do to me. He had not told me what he would do, when I walked upon him buying drugs. I just felt that whatever he was going to do would be bad. And what he did to me was bad. I was not a child who got whippings at home after Mama left home when I was about 3 years old. Although he had never been abusive toward me before, his personality had changed. I was convinced that he was serious about what he said.

I stayed home alone, despite my sisters' urging me to come along with them to Pickens. I paid a big price. I was overwhelmed with fear and started praying that they would come home early the minute it was sundown.

When it got dark, I got scared and got under the bed with an oil lamp and a book. It would take about 20 years later for me to realize how dangerous putting a lighted lamp under a bed was. Had the mattress caught fire, I would not have been able to stop the fire and the house would have burned down.

The next Saturday after the hours under the bed, when I was reluctant to go to Pickens, my sister told me "You are not staying at this house alone again tonight." I went to Pickens.

I listened to my sister's advice that I go to Pickens and not stay home alone again. It was a case of 'I'll be damned if I do, and I'll be damned if I don't.' The very minute that I stepped in Walter Body's with my sisters and friends, my boyfriend was there. He spotted me and immediately approached me swinging his fist. My sister, who had decided that she was my bodyguard for the night, stabbed my boyfriend in the back with a metal fingernail file. Then all I could remember is that everybody in the Honky-Tonk was fighting. I witnessed my first bar brawl, and I was the cause of it all.

I had a black eye. I was embarrassed to go to school on Monday as the swelling did not go away Sunday and my eye was very blood-shot and swollen. I did not want to stay home alone on Tuesday. Although my eye was still very black and blue, it was not very swollen. So, I went to school on Tuesday. I was more embarrassed about my appearance than I was in pain. I did not have a makeup to cover the bruised eye up. Gee, I was the High School Queen! I had to be perfect and well-groomed, I thought. I aspired to be the best High School Queen ever. I would be a great role model for the other students. I was an honor student and the Secretary of the Senior Class. I would later be Co-Valedictorian. Until this bar brawl happened, I was doing good. So far, none of the students knew about our charades in Pickens on Saturday Nights.

None of the students at school asked me about my black eye, although I already had an alibi. I was going to tell them that I had hit my head on the mantle, which was what I used when I got to my World History Class and the teacher asked me to stay after class. The teacher confronted me. He asked, "What happened to your eye?" I stated, "I hit it on the mantle." This highly respected teacher was a member of the American Legion. He knew a few things about survival. He countered my alibi with, "Looks like a fist to me." I did not argue. The teacher then asked if I had steak or an Irish Potato at home. I told him that I had an Irish Potato and he told me to cut the end of the potato off, leave the skin on and sleep with it on that night. He said that the blood would be drawn out the next morning and it was. I just have a scar as the result of the cut along my brow line. The teacher further instructed me to stay out of Pickens. I was surprised to learn that he knew that we went to Pickens on Saturday Nights. He lived in Canton, 25 miles away.

My boyfriend was from a very prominent family there in Pickens. We did not attend the same school. He attended a Catholic School. His father was not in the home. However, his mother did a respectable job of taking care of him and his brother. They obviously were spoiled. My boyfriend's mother was nice to me. She would let him drive her car to see me. She allowed me to spend the night. She made sure that I had nice clothes. The clothes were expensive, even though they were not new. I could wear the clothes. They were perfect fits and gave me a sophisticated grown-up look. She would give me Estee Lauder Youth Dew as presents. She did not know that I did not like the cologne because it reminded me of funerals. Mama would become emotional at funerals and hand me to other mourning women. Most of the women wore black and wore Estee Lauder. The women would not allow me to go back to Mama until the funeral was over, despite my whining and crying. Amazingly, I later became close with my college boyfriend's mother, and she gave me Estee Lauder Youth Dew perfume. The perfume always lasted a long time because you only needed to spray it once. It would penetrate your clothes and stay there for months.

The black eye ended my romance with the perpetrator. It caused me to experience a deep depression as I was smart enough to know that love should not hurt. I was just crushed. Had Daddy been alive, the guy would have been minced meat.

I also had friends in Pickens, who were willing to inform me of everything wrong that my boyfriend was doing. There was a girlfriend who attended the same Catholic School as he. There was also a girlfriend in Pickens, who was a friend of my catholic girlfriend. I was to learn later that my boyfriend was really using hard drugs and that he had become rowdy, participating in an orgy at the Honky-Tonk owner's house orchestrated by the drug dealing adopted daughter, that he had drawn a .22 caliber rifle on the mother and had wrecked her car, wrapping it around a tree. His mother had bought him the rifle for reasons I was not aware of. He was lucky to be alive after wrecking the car, but he was barely hurt.

My first love.

Because I did not live in Pickens and was busy with my life, school, and hairstyling, I would not see my boyfriend if he did not come to see me. I would just bump into him in Pickens, as I had when I ran into him doing the drug transaction. We did not have cell phones back then. My family did not have a phone anyway. Communication took place by gossip. Back then, the 'grapevine' was valuable, reliable, and needed. Otherwise, people would not mingle. The people in the black community needed to be able to interact with one another for the sake of survival.

This boy was my first love. He could have run a train through my nose, and it would not touch either side. I recall necking with him in poison oak and almost died from it. The poison oak was running up trees in a nice shady place in the woods. Neither of us knew what it was. We just thought it to be very inviting and a beautiful place to neck and hang out. He had left me when I started itching severely. I had a knot on my neck and my skin was broken out for over a week. The only thing that helped me was calamine lotion. All my exposed body had a rash from the poisonous plant. I was wearing a one-piece bathing suit. Luckily, we were out of school for the summer. Daddy had no idea how I got poison oak, and nobody was volunteering to tell him. Daddy just took me to the doctor when the knot formed on my neck. There were also blisters. My entire complexion changed to a darker shade.

I suppose I was a bit self-centered. I was not faithful to my main boyfriend. Although I was really in love with him, and I have not loved anyone as much as I loved him since then. I would talk with other boys. None of those other boys were able to get me to engage in sex. My main boyfriend had tried to go all the way on the day we were in the poison ivy. Luckily, he was a premature ejaculator. I did not get pregnant this one time we tried to have sex in the poison ivy. Using a condom never crossed either of our minds and it was not that neither of us did not know about condoms. We were just careless. Had I not been in denial thinking that I was the only one that he was having sex with, I might have insisted that he used one. Later, I was to learn through gossip that he was going to Vietnam and that he was getting married to another girl and that they would later have eleven children. I was flabbergasted and depressed! People did not mind sharing unsolicited information with you when they knew you had a crush or cared deeply for someone. Oftentimes, they just wanted to see if you would 'squirm.' I could not hide my hurt. I hurt too badly. I really was not the only one as I thought I was. This disappointment spearheaded my promiscuity. I decided that it was okay to consider dating other guys. Yet, none of them would replace the special place in my heart for my main boyfriend. I was clinically depressed. I just did not know how to get psychiatric care. I just learned to abuse alcohol once I was away in college shortly after. It was a Band-Aid.

The Hand Of God Was On My Life

I believe strongly that higher education and being remarkably busy figuring out survival helped me keep my sanity. My philosophy was that you either moved forward or you gave up and became a statistic. Quitting never crossed my mind. And I thank God that I never thought about quitting. The only way to go was forward and not backwards. There was nothing back there. Nothing. Daddy was gone. Mama had come back in body, but not in spirit. Mama had a motive, but it was not that she cared so much for us girls, but that she needed an income. And we were her source. Her demanding work in Cafes and whatever else she was doing when she was 'out there' was no longer sustaining her. My sisters were leaving Mississippi one by one. I barely noticed as time was moving on and I was focused on myself and not on what was happening around me. I had a good batting average.

I did not recognize that my survival was because the hand of God had always been on my life. I had heard the story over and over about how difficult it was for Mama to bring me into this world. But somehow, I always felt that I would be okay. Figuring out the logistics of getting to school daily and getting to Upward Bound on Saturdays kept my mind occupied. I was an 'A' student, 'Miss Velma Ware Jackson High' and co-valedictorian. There was no room for fear and depression. I handled my business without the help of others.

I remember coming home from my Junior High School Prom to an empty house at 11 PM. I was not fazed by the fact that Mama was not there. I did not want my date to know that I was home alone. There were a few other incidents where I recognized that I was not safe, but I handled them in stride and nothing bad happened. I routinely got up the next morning and got myself off to school.

One of the incidents happened one Saturday Evening when I was on my way home from Upward Bound. The bus driver would stop for about 30 minutes in Canton and then go on to Pickens. Students could get off the bus for a quick break. I decided that I needed to go to the restroom. I ducked into a tavern near to the bus. I noticed that there were two women and a man in the front of the tavern at the bar area. One woman was sweeping, and the other woman and the man were sitting on barstools. They glanced at me and kept talking. One of the women was sweeping around the bar. I was urgent and ran to the back to use the toilet. Nobody warned me to stop. I was in position to relieve myself and looked up into the face of a woman propped against the wall by the commode. I noticed that she was dead because she had a butcher knife sticking out of her very pregnant stomach up near her heart. When I realized what I was looking at, I no longer needed to relieve myself. I ran out of the tavern. The people at the front of the tavern just looked at me as if nothing was wrong. I noticed that the woman who was sweeping had stopped and the three of them were now huddled. I got on the bus and did not talk about what had happened. I was obviously in shock. It did not occur to me until later that I could have been framed for the murder. I kept my ears open and learned the next week by reading a newspaper that the mother died, but the baby lived. Ironically, the deceased woman's last name was Slaughter.

As time moved on, I was shocked into reality the day that school was out in my junior year. I was the last child at home. I would have to wait a week or so before I was to go to Upward Bound for the summer. I went home and waited for Mama to show up. When it was about sundown, I realized that I really was home alone, and that Mama was not coming home that night. Reality also shocked me when I realized that my last sister at home was off to St. Louis with my neighbor her age. They would go to Job Corps there. My sister went to live with two older sisters, who were willing to help her get a start in life. Mama's second oldest daughter was our connection in St. Louis.

Although Mama's second oldest daughter did not live with us in Goodman, Mississippi, she was Mama's second daughter from another marriage. She visited us occasionally in Mississippi. She would play with me a lot. She would aggravate me when I was about two years old when she would try to make me speak properly. I would ask for bed when I meant that I wanted bread. I came to like her a bit more as I grew older. At age 9, I asked her if I could visit her and she said, "yes". I really enjoyed my summer in St. Louis. I recall being very naïve. We did not use bad language back then and the word, funk or funky were considered bad words. I traveled to St. Louis on Continental Trailways Bus. It did not bother me that we would stop in every little town on the route to St. Louis. It was interesting to me that someone would post the word "Funks" along the corn crops that extended for miles along the route. I would get tickled and loudly laugh every time I saw the word. A man sitting across from me was puzzled that I was so tickled. He stared at me for a long period of time because the signs kept popping up and I could not control my laughter. I safely made it to St. Louis where my sister and her boyfriend, who drove a taxicab met me.

There were no cell phones in 1959. I wonder even now how people were able to communicate so well. I have made a mental note that people were more accountable back then, than people are today. My sister did not have children. She would take me everywhere she went, besides work. My sister would have her play mother babysit me days when she went to work. The play mother had an adopted daughter about a year younger than me. The daughter was spoiled and quite streetwise. She showed me around St. Louis. Her mother was a homebody, who constantly asked us to stay within perimeters she had set up, but her daughter always managed to venture outside those perimeters. Although my sister was not able to take us out on field trips and camps, she would pay for me to go with the play sister to places such as Chuck Berry's home, Grants' Farm and the Monsanto YMCA. I enjoyed going to Meramec Caverns and to Busch Wildlife in Louisiana, Missouri for fishing. I enjoyed my first trip so much that I asked to visit my sister again when I became thirteen years old. She agreed, probably because she wanted to appease me after the loss of Daddy. My play sister and I went to Monsanto YMCA weekdays so that my play sister's mother could have some peace. My play sister was getting even more streetwise. This time we would venture farther away from home. My play sister's family was in the De 'Ville Neighborhood here in St. Louis. On any good day, we might end up in Wellston. This girl knew her way around. Once we were told to go to visit my sister's cousin across town somewhere. My play sister decided that she wanted Chop Suey. Of course, I followed her and somewhere along our route on Eastern Avenue, we ran into a gang doing a drill. We became frightened and began to run. I almost fainted because every alley we came to for about three blocks, the gangsters ran out in front of us, and we had to stop and allow them to pass. We were trembling. I thought I would faint, but the gangsters acted as though we did not phase them. They kept drilling. This was also the day of a total eclipse of the sun and moon at noon. Yes, we were still not where we were supposed to be at Noon. Luckily, we arrived at my cousin's house before my sister showed up after work. She had no clue as to what we had been up to.

My play sister and I were growing up. However, she was outgrowing me. She had begun to like boys and I had not met the young man that would later become my babysitter when Callie needed a sitter. When we went to the YMCA, Callie would pack us a brown bag lunch. She would put two sandwiches in one bag. My play sister and I would take turns carrying the bag each day. One day when it was her turn to carry the lunch, she did not want to carry it. I sat the bag on the ground. She and I both walked away from the bag and before we could walk two or three strides away, a kid ran by very fast, snatched up the bag and we did not see him or our lunch again. Now we were hungry all day. To make matters worse, I thought I was doing something telling Callie what had happened with the lunch. I soon found out that telling Callie was not a good choice. Callie decided that she would no longer be packing a lunch for us and that she was not giving any lunch money to us.

I learned even more about my play sister's craftiness. One day about the close of the day camp, I walked past the soda machine, which took a large number of nickels because a soda was fifteen cents. I noticed that my play sister was beckoning me to come there. She had tied a large number of nickels in her shirttail. She needed me to put nickels in my shirttail as well. I did what she said do. When the teacher learned what had happened, she did not make us turn the money in. I thought this was strange. But I soon thought, oh well. It was later in life that I learned that teachers were not always fair in judgment.

When Callie learned that we girls were getting too rough, she stopped paying for us to go to the YMCA. She decided that I would have a male babysitter, a couple years my senior. I really liked him. He was in Beaumont High School and the son of a police officer. He would date me, take me to his home in Richmond Heights to visit his family and believe it or not, he was a total gentleman. The only concern about his not being an angel is that he smoked cigarettes. We would walk around in Forest Park, in Gas Light Square evenings or hang out on the balcony at Callie's apartment. On the balcony, we would spy on the girl and the boy across the street, who were sitting on the balcony necking. I do not remember my babysitter and I doing any necking. When we visited his home and would go to the back of the house to be alone, we always were haunted by his younger brother and his sister. His brother would try to traumatize me. He would look for things to ridicule me about. When I returned home to Goodman, Mississippi, I would receive the sweetest love letters from him. He sent me a picture that I have to this day. I lost track of him somewhere among my busyness. I have tried to find him since I moved to St. Louis in 1986. I have had no luck in my search.

My sister Barbara Nell came to St. Louis with me a year or so later when they were putting the top on the Arch. Barbara Nell, my play sister and I walked from Newberry Terrace to the Riverfront to witness the Event. Although the workers did not successfully place the top on the Arch that day, it was a spectacular viewing seeing the cranes up atop of the Arch trying to place that final piece to the puzzle. We should have waited until the next day because the workers were successful the next day. Again, I had a good time visiting St. Louis. Despite my enjoyment of the visits, I always knew that I had to go back home to Mississippi. I never dreamed that I would end up living in St. Louis.

Early on in life, I had learned to fight to defend myself. I had a cousin, Bettie Jean, who would visit sometimes. We would fight by biting each other's bottom lips. We were about two years old. I also had to fight my sibling rival, Barbara Nell, who never got over the fact that she was not the baby. She was two years older than me. We were teenagers when we had our last fight. I had to hit her 'with all of my might' to get her off me. That was our last entanglement. I could see that I had hurt her with the punch I threw her that time. Her love for me was awkward. She did not mind beating the stuffing out of me, but she would not allow anybody else to beat me up. As I mentioned earlier, she was the one who defended me from my abusive boyfriend. Barbara Nell was also active in my defense when we had the fight on the school bus.

The fight on the school bus was my first education as to how attractive I had become as a young woman. I was not aspiring for a boyfriend then because I was still under the impression that my first lover and I were going to have a future. So, it did not bother me to move over so that the young man had asked if he could sit next to me on the bus. I did not think about the fact that he was usually sitting next to the regular bus driver's daughter on the front seat. I assumed that he sat there most of the time because he was the first stop. He was from Up North, which is what we called Chicago and Kansas City at that time. He dressed neatly. But he really was not that appealing to me. When the bus driver's daughter got on the bus, she challenged me for my seat. Today my nephew was driving the bus. He was new at it. He just drove the bus and allowed us students to fight. It was a terrible fight. I was startled to see that most of the students practically were fighting. I was extremely shocked to see my sister Stella was fighting because she had me under the impression that she was afraid of everything. Well I could have been wrong as this girl was so likeable that everyone tried to defend her. Anyhow, she came to my rescue and I was glad. One of the opposite team was on top of me and she was biting my finger. She practically bit my finger off. I had to give her a black eye and Stella pulled her off me. I luckily only lost my fingernail. It never occurred to me that I should have had medical attention to ward off rabies. The feud between the two families was very real. A day or so after the fight, I was caught walking alone in the hallway at school when the girl who bit my finger and her friends were also in the hallway. Somehow The girl thought she had support of her friends and attacked me again. I immediately defended myself, grabbed her by her skirt, gave her a jab and she twirled away from me all the way to the end of the hall, three classrooms away from where I had hit her. When she noticed that I still had her skirt in my hand, she had to come back to me to get loose. I was amazed at my skill and power. I felt that I was a magician. I had not practiced or done anything like that before.

There were consequences. The principal got word of the fighting. We both were whipped by the principal. I was more embarrassed than hurt from the whipping as the principal was lecturing me all the while he was whipping me. I could hear him say, "Miss Jackson High, I am disappointed with you fighting." I thought this was the end of the fighting to find out later that my niece my age was attacked a day or so later after my bus stop. She could not defend herself as she was attacked by the feuding family because she was alone and her siblings on the bus were too young to understand that they needed to fight to defend her. I am not clear as to who was driving the bus that day. I do not know if it was my niece's older brother or the regular bus driver, the father of the feuding girls. I learned much later in life that my nephew was concerned about losing his job had he intervened. We were all immature and inexperienced. We had not learned to love one another by protecting one another. Our philosophies seemed to be that if you did not have the same last name or you did not live next door, you were the enemy. Yet we had not grasped the Swahili principle of harambee. My philosophy was that if you did not bother me, I would not bother you. But if you bothered me, you were as good as dead. I had the right to eliminate you as you were trying to eliminate me.

I was not suspended from school for fighting. The punishment by the principal took care of the fighting on both sides. Back in the 1960's, children did not fight with weapons a lot as children do now. If you could not win a fight with your brawn, the other man just won the fight.

Poverty is a State of Mind

Mama and I continued to live in the family home after all of the other children had gone. I needed to complete my high school education. I was not a quitter. And I saw that I had no other decent options other than to continue my education. On one occasion when I was in the 12th grade, I learned that Mama was no longer living in our home, that she had moved in with our cousin Lucy. I somehow got the word that I was to live with Mama and our Cousin Lucy that year. I would go to my cousin's house after school and I remember living with the two of them for a short time. Then I got the news that Cousin Lucy's house had burned down and that all of my keepsakes in my trunk were burned too. I was devastated that I had lost my stuff. I was not too worried about where I would live because I was aware that I had been accepted to attend Tougaloo College and that I would have a full grant to pay for my tuition, room and board and my books. I also had work study provided by the college. Mama would continue to get the Social Security Check for me because I was still a student. I did not get that money because there was no way for Mama and I to communicate really.

On the Tougaloo College Campus, we were all just students. Nobody looked down on the economic status of others. I was sociable and blended in well with the haves and the have nots. When I completed the Upward Bound Program, I would go directly into college somewhere in September.

I went to my grandparents' home to visit Mama during the break before the Fall Semester was to begin at Tougaloo. I did some deep thinking during the several days I as there. I would have no future there and nobody tried to keep me there. I would have to go to school or go to work and there was no work in Camden.

I had only applied to two colleges: Tougaloo College and Tennessee State University. I was enrolled in Tougaloo for a month before I heard from Admissions at Tennessee State University telling me that I had been accepted there. I decided to stay enrolled in Tougaloo, at least I knew that I had a full ride there and that I would not have to go through a lot of changes. Survival was physically and mentally draining. My ego was also bruised by the late response. Afterall, Tennessee State did not know who they were dealing with. I was co-valedictorian of my senior class, Miss Jackson High, cute and popular. I had a large amount of pride, despite my level of poverty. I traveled freely and alone, handled my own money which was no more than $80 a month from my work study. I kept my head high. I dreamed big dreams.

Now that I look back, I was hell bent on attending Tennessee State because I wanted to get revenge against one of my most respected teachers, who had made a snide remark when he asked me where I was going to attend college. When I told him that I was going to attend Tennessee State, he said, "You'll be pregnant by the time you've been there two weeks." I was going to make a liar out of him. Well, I did not go to Tennessee State, but I never got over the teacher's remark. I had already learned that teachers were not perfect because many of them were sexually abusing students. Of course, I did not think that I was sexually abused by the teacher that I was having sex with. I did not know my value and thought it an honor to be noticed by the male teacher. Although I was not in love with the teacher, the brief affair helped me get over my first love. The teacher was only a couple of years older than me. He had graduated early from high school and college. He was related to the Principal. I had no idea that I was not the only student that he was having sex with. I came to know that he was having sex with many of the girls. He had sex with my cousin, who did not know he was having sex with me. He had sex with a lower classman, got her pregnant and was forced to marry her. The teacher was very smart. He taught courses that I was not strong in. I was grateful to be able to get the 'A' that he gave me. He was very helpful to Mama and me. When he would come to visit, he would chop wood for the fireplace. Mama liked him. Our relationship was not to be. I also was not to be pregnant because we did not practice safe sex. Condoms never came up. Actually, we did not talk a lot. We had sex at home. Mama was always present.

God Hid Me

Unfortunately, my promiscuous behavior was an act that I was copying from my older siblings and the older adults around me. Promiscuity became a part of my value system. I had no remorse about having sex when it happened. Rarely was it so great that I would form a soul tie. Most of the boyfriends I had were very nice and did not bring up the subject of sex. A brief kiss goodnight was all that was required of me from most of them. This promiscuity went all the way with me into college, where I met the first man who decided that we would get married. This young man was a fellow student. He proposed. We even had engagement rings. The young man was so nice and excited to have me as his girlfriend. I was vulnerable and allowed him and another female student convince me to cut my hair and wear it as an Afro. The other photo was my press, curl and finger wave hairstyle.

My College photo

Man I almost married in college

This photo is me in my Senior year in high school.

I wore the afro with pride. My fiancé loved it. We were getting along fine. He helped me change my hair from straight to the Afro.

One day I was offered the proposition of becoming an exchange student at Dartmouth College. I was told that all my expenses would be paid.

My fiancé did not approve of my leaving Tougaloo. I insisted that I take the opportunity to study at Dartmouth. During the process of his mother trying to console him to keep him mentally and emotionally stable, she encouraged him to let me go. The fact that I could go without a huge amount of remorse is that I had learned that while I greatly admired my fiancé's mother, I really was not in love to the extent that I could not separate from him for a year and be as devastated as I was after my first love did not work out. I did not believe that I could ever get over losing my first love.

I never asked my fiancé if I was his first love. He would take me to his home on weekends just as I did with my first love. I would spend a couple of nights and we would return to campus on Sunday evenings. I got along well with his family, just like I did with the first love's family. The fiancé's mother gave me Estee Lauder Youth Dew for presents, just like my first love's mother did. This gesture was one of the confirmations that she cared for me. His younger sister also took me in stride.

My fiancé was determined that he would pledge the fraternity, Omega Psi Phi. He was the take charge type. He encouraged me to pledge Delta Sigma Theta Sorority, the Sister Sorority. I pledged Delta. I was Duck #1in Line. I made it across the Burning Sands.

The logic for my leaving my fiancé was that I needed to ensure that I graduated from school, had the finances to do so, and I was uncertain as to whether I should be getting married right away either. My fiancé nor myself had no independent incomes at the time. I was not a student of faith, I was a candidate of survival, which was all I knew at the time.

When things are going too well for me, they will soon change. I had a paradigm shift. I was offered an opportunity in my Sophomore year to be an exchange student. I was informed that all tuition would be paid for me to go along with three other schoolmates to Dartmouth College in New Hampshire for a year.

I was invited by one of the other students, at that time, my best friend. to come with her to New York City to live with her aunt in the Bronx for the summer before going to school at Dartmouth in the Fall. We would get jobs and pay for our food. I was more than obliged to have been given such an opportunity to visit New York.

Things were going well for me. I worked at the Federal Reserve Bank in Manhattan as a Summer Hire in the Mint Department. I was able to see gold bricks from different countries. It took a long time for me to understand that my desk was located on the floor next to these gold bricks and that meant high security. There were no incidences back in 1970. I now feel grateful now that there were no domestic terrorist activities in the 1970's.

I was the assistant to the receptionist. I did not have to work, so getting to work on time was the most stressful thing that I had to do daily.

I had a great time in New York. It did not bother the three of us that we lived in a small apartment with one king sized bed. We all stayed out nights, came home at sunrise, took showers, dressed, and left for work. There was no hands-on supervision because the aunt was young, popular and a student at New York City College. She took a vacation to St. Thomas, Virgin Islands for about two weeks. My friend and I had the flexibility to do whatever we wanted. I soon learned after arriving in New York City that there were trains that went in different directions, and I soon caught on to that. I traveled independently thereafter.

I was an exchange student from Tougaloo College in Tougaloo, MS to Dartmouth College in Hanover, NH in the 1970-71 school year. I was in my junior year when I arrived at Dartmouth. I was one of three other African American Females from my home school. We were to go back to Tougaloo to graduate after one year. We were not informed that that there was another option: to graduate from Dartmouth. This pilot cohort was successful. It was my understanding that there were about 85 females on campus. Most of the other females on Campus were Caucasian. I believe I was able to witness a few female students of Native American descent, who were housed in another dormitory, away from the dormitory where the other female students lived. The female students were basically segregated. I still have difficulty understanding why this cohort was not allowed to graduate from Dartmouth. I believe that had there been a greater effort to socialize the different female races, the conversation of why the 1970-71 Cohort was not allowed to go back to Dartmouth and finish their senior year would not be happening today, fifty years later.

My major was psychology. My favorite subjects at Dartmouth were in psychology and Drama. One course in psychology that stood out to me was the trust formation course where students were taught to accept others of cultural difference. I dated a Caucasian student named Jim. Jim was in trust formation class. I learned that Jim was living with a couple in the White Mountains in J. D. Salinger's old home. Had I known that I was venturing into the mountains, I probably would have turned down the date. Jim and I left Dartmouth Campus at 6 pm, stopped at the country store in the valley and bought some wheat germ and other health foods. I had no idea that this is what dinner would consist of. It as a far cry from soul food. I chose not to eat the food. I did partake of the marijuana. When we arrived at Jim's home, it was after 9 pm. I cannot figure out why the large lapse in time. Either Jim lived a long way from the campus, or his 1948 Ford Truck was rolling very slowly on the unpaved roads. I did not realize that time would go so fast. I also found it strange that when I arrived back on campus, it was around noon the next day. This is one of those times that I ventured off and did not have any idea of where I was going. Luckily, Jim was nice enough to stop trying to neck with me when I let him know that I did not want to neck.

I also enjoyed playing the Froggy in a Caribbean Play taught by Professor Errol Hill. The play was well-publicized. as I recall the New York Times Newspaper found it noteworthy. I probably would have thought I was a real star, noteworthy of pay had I not forgotten a couple of lines on the last night, when one of the directors, a student gave me a marijuana joint. I became confused and had to be given a clue to continue the drama. Froggy was the narrator of the story.

I was not prepared in any way for the different environment that I was venturing into. Nobody had told me anything. The teacher, who recruited me for the program did not discuss the purpose of sending us students into this environment. I was to figure this out on my own after I was knee-deep into the situation. I figured that I was supporting the Feminist Movement. I finally did agree to go into this unchartered territory. I had nothing to lose and possibly something to gain. Had I left; I would have been out of school with no financial aid. As a female in an all-male predominately Caucasian environment, I had many challenges to overcome. The winters were extremely cold and there was just too much snow. There was no travel by automobile during the winter months. I learned what it was like to be an Inuk and how it is to live in Alaska where there is six months of night. The year began and ended before I could experience the six months of daylight. Two of the other African American students and I did not like the cafeteria food. We bought a hot plate and kept our juice and milk on the window – sills for refrigeration. It worked. I enjoyed the campus until the snow came.

Absence Makes the Heart Grow Fonder

I did find love on the Dartmouth Campus. I became fascinated by one African American Upperclassman. I had a chemistry with that guy. I learned that the upperclassman was off to another country to continue his master's Program. I was forced to assume that the relationship was over based on the need for him to complete his schooling, which painted a promising future. I had noticed that the upperclassman did not do a lot of talking to me about his plans. He just told me that he was a Rhodes Scholar and that he would be going to Oxford in England. He suggested to me that I should go with him to England, but He did not say anything else about it. I said nothing. Another guy had suggested that I go with him to Canada. I could not see myself leaving the country and I had not finished school. I was adamant that I would finish college. I did not feel secure about leaving the country. However, had the upperclassman that I had the chemistry with said that he had enough money to take care of me and himself while we were away, I probably would have bought his suggestion. Other than my degree, I did not have anything to lose. He just did not share enough information to convince me. I knew that I would need money. He did not do enough talking and we did not have cellphones back then. I mentally distanced myself from the guy who was off to England and I had already moved on in my mind when he came to visit me over the Summer in Atlanta.

I had forgotten about the fiancé that I had left back at Tougaloo. I felt that the relationship was going nowhere, despite our engagement with rings. When we told his mother that I was going to Dartmouth and she did not seem approve, I came to know years later that she, like any mother would do, tried to give her son hope and was helping him to let me go. I also suspected that my fiancé had found out that I was seeing another guy at Dartmouth. The 'Gmolestationvine' was strong back then. I learned that my fiancé was seeing my younger sorority sister. Once back on campus, I also came to know that they would be getting married. The Gmolestationvine was intense at Tougaloo too. I do not recall having any violent break up with my fiancé. There was no fight. When I returned to campus, I noticed that he did not come looking for me. I saw that the fiancé and I just stopped communicating. I had no problem moving on when I arrived back at Tougaloo to complete my senior year. I dated another student for a minute. There was no chemistry there. We were just hanging out waiting for graduation day.

Although I liked the young man that I was dating at Dartmouth a lot, I could not see a future there as he was off to Europe. Although he had mentioned that I could join him there, he was did not give me any details as to how I was supposed to survive financially. I had no idea that he would have enough money to take care of both of us. Years later, I was to learn that he was just shy. While it was spilled milk, I was better able to bring closure to the relationship that was not to be. Another thought was foremost in my mind. I was just entering my senior year and I needed to graduate.

My interaction with faculty at Dartmouth, other than with Professor Errol Hill, was minimal. Professor Hill was over the Drama Department there. I was lead actor in a play, "T'Jean and His Brothers", a Caribbean Drama. In other words, I was without counseling. I often wonder now what my options were now that I have knowledge that after I left Dartmouth to go back to Tougaloo to graduate, that the next year's female exchange students were able to graduate from Dartmouth.

A year later, back at Tougaloo College, the four of us exchange students learned that we had no provision for room and board. However, we persevered, and we all graduated.

A Winner Never Quits and a Quitter Never Wins

Two of us ex-exchange students were now back at Tougaloo at the mercy of another of us who could sublet her sister's apartment off campus. Things were going well until the last semester. The student, who was in charge of the apartment found herself getting married. That means that the other two of us were forced to move out. I was forced to hide out in the dormitory with students who knew of my plight and tried to help me. The Dorm Matron would check to ensure that all of the girls were in and that there were no boys in the building. Boys were not allowed past the Dorm Matron's Station. Somehow the Dorm Matron, who was good at her job noticed that I was in the dorm and that I should not have been there. She would walk the halls calling my name. I would not respond. She would get tired and go to bed herself. I was determined that I would remain in school. I asked the school secretary's daughter, who was a student living in Jackson, off campus to allow me to live with her and she agreed. I was there for about a week and was told that I could not live there. I was not aware of having done anything to cause me to have to go, other than being myself. Maybe it was that I had pledged Delta Sigma Theta and the student I was living with had pledged Alpha Kappa Alpha, my rival sorority. I was then back to hiding out in the dorm with a couple of sympathetic students.

It finally occurred to me that I had a sister-in-law in Jackson. My brother, who was deceased, had left her with four children, three of who were still at home. I visited and told her of my plight. She allowed me to live there and sleep in the bunk bed above her daughter. I might have been living there two weeks when one night around 9 PM, I went out on the balcony to hang my panty hose on the line to dry and observed my sister-in-law in the car with her Caucasian lover necking. While I was a bit shocked, I went back into the house and went to bed. The next day after I returned from school and my sister-in-law came home from work, she told me that I could no longer stay there. I was highly disappointed this time about being evicted because I thought that I was set until graduation. The niece and nephews were getting along fine. I was bonding with them. I had no idea what she told them regarding my having to leave as I had a little money from work study and could feed myself. I only ate one meal daily, a practice I had formed during high school. I weighed about 126 pounds.

I ran into the other ex-exchange student who lived with us in the subleased apartment. She had found housing and work study at a halfway house. She and the other ex-exchange student were already living at the halfway house. I was exhausted by now and was severely depressed. I would attempt to relieve my depression by sleeping and taking my roommate's Darvon pills that she used to treat her epilepsy. I was sleeping days. I remember one day I she awakened me and told me that the student at Dartmouth that I had the great chemistry with and had tried to force out of my mind, had come by to see me and that she had told him that I was asleep. She was the motherly type, the oldest of her siblings and this is how she treated us other students, despite her being our classmate. I also thought that she had another motive as well, based on something I had learned while we were at Dartmouth. She also had knowledge that this man would not be a good pick for me as she had introduced me to her homeboy, who I ended up getting married to later in life. She did not try to wake me up until my Knight In shining Armor was back in his car driving down the street. She did not think that we were a good match. We did not have cell phones in the 1960's. I could not call him to turn around and come back. I had developed an intense stronghold for this young man, and he had gotten away. I was able to share this with him when I tracked him down 45 years later. He probably did not believe me when I told him that this had happened. He also sounded unbelievable to me when he told me that he was shy, 45 years later. This cat and mouse game convinced me that some relationships are not to be. We both were innocently immature. We had no idea that we were shaping our destinies. I informed the young man that had I followed him to Oxford England, he would not have reached his destiny, meaning that he would not have become a corporate lawyer. I figure now that we would have had so many babies that he would have had to go to work to feed us and forget about his schooling. My logic is that he is the youngest of 13 children and I am the youngest of 16. We had no plans to practice safe sex. Neither had we discussed planned parenthood.

So, I had learned to put another man out of my mind by burying him in my subconscious. I just moved on to the next and made the most of the relationship. Having a boyfriend was just something to do.

I was clinically depressed and traumatized by the disappointment that I faced arriving back at Tougaloo and learning that I was homeless. I was depressed, had visited with Mississippi's only African American Psychiatrist, who prescribed 5mg Valium 2 X daily back in my Sophomore year. I am sure that I was not taking the pills as prescribed, and the doctor did not check my medications. I just happened to be one of her students. I had learned to mask my ailment. I had an incident of drowsiness once and missed the bed by about five feet, thinking that I was getting into the bed when I was in the hotel in Atlanta. I was alone when the incident happened. The medication needed to be checked by a doctor. Luckily when I ran out of the pills, I did not refill the prescription. I could have had a serious accident. I did not know that 10 mg of Valium is a high dosage.

I was studying psychology and to me, Abnormal Psychology was just another course. I needed to graduate and would not graduate without it. I do remember experiencing the feeling that many of the defense mechanisms and diagnoses listed many symptoms that I had. On the Bachelor Level, students were not privy to the DSM, (Diagnostic Statistical Manual). I now know that I was depressed. My work experience in social work taught me that I might have continued treatment had I known the severity of my diagnosis. As my lifestyle improved, I became much less depressed as I met a new man, and I was happily in love. I was sleeping in hotpants at our apartment in Jackson when my roommate with the maternal instincts introduced me to this very handsome, flirtatious young man from Indiana. We connected right away. He returned to Indiana as he was just visiting my roommate as a family friend. We had exchanged phone numbers and conversed for hours at a time. I was to learn later that he was also from my roommate's hometown Greenwood, MS. He was just a couple of years older than me. He finally asked me to visit his family in Michigan City, Indiana when I had Spring Break. He was already working fulltime in finance, still living at his father's home. Money was no object for him. He was willing to pay my fare to visit him. I visited my newly found love, met his family, and blended in well. They were highly sociable in the Indiana high society, well known, having friends extending from Michigan City, Indiana to South Bend, Indiana, to Gary, Indiana to Chicago, Illinois. When there was a party, which spanned over the entire weekend, people from all these places were on the invitation list. Milwaukee, Wisconsin and Minneapolis, Indiana were sometimes on the list. I came to know that this side of my friend's family was his father's mother's side and later learned that his mother lived in Los Angeles, California. I would not meet her until later in our relationship. I came to know, however that his mother played an active role in his life. She was more like his older sister because she had him when she was a teenager. I also came to know that his maternal grandmother had raised him and a brother just nine months younger than he. Both the paternal and the maternal families were originally from Greenwood, Mississippi. I learned that my lover would spend the school year in Greenwood and summers in Michigan City with his father. Not being a big conversationalist, I did not question him much about his past. I later came to know that I really did not know much about his past at all nor about his lifestyle other than the fact that he was a party animal, quite different from the popularity of other boys that I had dated.

My new lover was more worldly and mature. I was yet to learn that he had a lot of baggage too. He was a party animal, frequenting night clubs on the caliber of The Playboy Club in Chicago and other bars and taverns. He treated me like I was a queen. I can say that I was in love with him. It appeared to be so natural that upon my graduation from Tougaloo, my Knight in Shining Armor was there to whisk me away to Atlanta.

I had once more found love and I would not be leaving him, not for a while anyway.

His uncle had driven down with him for the graduation. We parted ways with the uncle when we got to Atlanta.

I played flute, alto saxophone, and bass clarinet in high school. One of my sisters gifted me with a flute for my graduation from college. I recall lying on the top of Lookout Mountain playing the flute during the trip to Atlanta.

We lived in a hotel in Downtown Atlanta for about a week. He got a job and we moved into an apartment in College Park, Georgia.

I soon got a job working for the Bank of Atlanta for a year or so. We were happy there in College Park. Marriage never crossed either of our minds. We were just living carefree. We got along fine just as we were.

I attempted to try to do the chores of a wife a couple of times. I tried to cook cabbage one day, got nude and went to sleep with the pot on the stove in the daytime.

I was sleeping very soundly when the thought came into my head, 'you'd better get up. You're sleeping too good.' While I was asleep, I went into this white tunnel. At one point in the tunnel was a man waving to me to come on down. It was very bright down there. The man looked very mature. He was dressed in all white, including his hat. I wanted to go down there. I had a strong urgency to go, thinking that he was Daddy's daddy, who I had never met. My granddaddy had died before I was born. Had not the warning thought come to my mind; I would have gone down there.

I awakened and less than twelve inches above my head, there was a cloud of smoke so thick that you could not see anything in the room. The tunnel was smoke going into my nostrils. I had to run outside and gasp for air. I was naked. My neighbors. people were looking over the balcony from upstairs. One of the men yelled, "Is everything okay down there?" I gasped for air and realized that I was naked and that there was a pot on the stove about to go up in flames. The smoke inhalation was bad enough for me to go to the doctor. But I just did not go to the doctor, despite my aching ribs. I did not tell my fiancé' what had happened. I am sure he figured it out.

On another occasion, I was home, and he was at work. I decided that I would do laundry. Today, I was going to make sure that I got rid of all those wine stains that were on his neckties. My daddy did not wear suits and ties. He wore khakis and a shirt. I had no idea that neckties were made of silk and that you had to dry clean them or the cotton would swell, and you could not iron it flat again. My fiancé had over one hundred of them. I threw all of them in the washing machine. I noticed that when I took them out of the dryer, the cotton was inside out and swelled up. I tried to get the cotton tucked back into the ties before he got home from work. I noticed that the part was damp where the cotton was. I tucked as much of the cotton back into the ties as I could and laid them on the bed. The rest I left in the laundry basket until I could get to them. I thought that he would be happy that I had washed his neckties.

I called him at work and said, "Honey, I washed your ties." His response was, "You washed my ties?", in a sarcastic and surprised manner. I did not realize that I had committed a horrible act until later that night when he was stuffing the cotton back into the ties, trying to iron then flat and talking to his grandmother on the phone. I heard him say, "And do you know that she washed my ties?"

When he got off the phone, I said, "And what does that mean? And do you know that she washed my ties?" It still had not occurred to me that I had messed up until then. He said, "You really don't know do you? You do not wash ties." I asked, "Then what do you do with them when they are stained and dirty like yours are?" He said, "You take them to the dry cleaners." I said, "Oh." It was then that I was relieved of my laundry duties for him. I was to learn later after we were married that the laundry issue meant a lot to him when he sent me to his Paternal Grandmother's home to have her teach me how to do laundry. I spent the entire day with her, and she did not teach me anything. She did the laundry herself. I watched television.

My fiancé soon learned that I was not to be left home alone after I had a couple of accidents around the house. I needed to go to work.

I had two jobs while I was in Atlanta. I found my first job on my own, working in Bookkeeping at The Bank of Atlanta. I was enjoying working there when most of the employees in my department, Accounts payable were laid off. My fiancé helped me get another job shortly thereafter at General Finance. I was enjoying working there. I worked there until I ended up leaving Atlanta. All the older experienced workers were very nice to me. Again, I was the token black. The most repulsive thing about that job was that the Caucasian manager would call me "Sunshine". He thought it to be a great pet name for me. Obviously, he did not know anything about Tougaloo and its culture. He did not know that the Tougaloo students of the Class of '72 was intolerant of anything sounding racist. I did not tell him that the Class of '72 had built a bond fire and burned our books because the Caucasian teacher from Harvard teaching Afro American Literature was teaching low self-esteem to the class. I remember reading one of the books describing the black girl from the Appalachians named Betsy. The book stated that among other things, Betsy's nose was so big and wide that when it rained, the raindrops would fall into her nostrils and a train could run through and never touch the sides. After the bond fire, which was over six feet high with the books, the teacher and the faculty got the message. The teacher left campus during the night and did not come back. The faculty warned us that Ford Foundation would take our money away for such an act. I did not hear any more about the incident and the Afro American Course took a more positive direction.

On another occasion, I was home alone reading a "Do it yourself section in the Reader's Digest Magazine". I read that you could clean your record albums with coca cola. and get the scratches off. I Did this and rinsed them, laid them out on newspaper to dry. When they seemed to be dry, I placed them back on top of each other to put in the sleeves later. We had a great collection of jazz, pop, rhythm and blues albums. When he came home to play some music, he learned that the albums were stuck together. The labels peeled off. He had to play each album and use a magic marker to write the artist and the songs on paper that he had cut out. He played music for a long time. It took over a week of constant music playing including the weekends to complete that chore. I was running around acting like Seeley in 'The Color Purple' when she was in trouble or being nosey and snickering.

By now, his father's family had accepted me without question. They just knew that we would be coming back to Indiana and getting married.

My fiancé suggested that I learned to drive. I learned to drive his standard shift Opal. One weekend I went shopping in his car and had an accident because I was driving too fast. New drivers like to speed. I was driving 80 MPH and decided at the spur of the minute that I wanted to exit the highway at the next ramp that I was too close to exit at that speed. It was an elevated ramp with a strip mall having a theater below. Before I was aware, I tried to brake, and the car was airborne. I landed in a row of cars causing the cars to fishtail and damage each other. Seeing that I had smashed up some property, I would have left the scene of the accident had my car not been disabled. Two men were leaving the theater talking and saw the accident. They went back into the theater and told the crowd. The people came out of the theater. I must have gotten home in a taxi because my friend was the only one of us who had a vehicle. I had to thank God that I was still alive. I only noticed that my ribcage had hit the steering wheel. I could see that the experience I had riding my family's mule when I was a child paid off. I held onto the steering wheel and was not ejected from the vehicle. When I looked up at the theatre Marquee, I saw that the movie was 'Five on the Black Hand Side.' I thought that it was ironic that such many Caucasian people would watch a black exploitation movie in Georgia. Afterall, it was a comedy. I came to know that the vehicle I was driving was not insured. My friend told me that the insurance had expired at midnight. I believed that he was just negligent and did not pay the insurance. We went to court. The defendants were ferocious. However, in the state of Georgia, the type of insurance was comparative. Each auto owner would pay his own damages. My friend somehow convinced me that I could buy a new car under the new graduate rule that auto dealerships had. I purchased a 1973 Toyota Corolla.

I became nervous when I learned that I had to go to court. I called my sister in Chicago, who decided that I would be leaving Georgia and coming to Chicago after learning that my fiancé's vehicle was not insured. I also believed that I needed to leave Georgia because my fiancé, who was popular, had begun to allow his friends from Mississippi to come and live with us in our guest bedroom. I did not like to socialize with many people. And living with them was out of the question. These people were his brother and his best friend from High School. I was a functioning depressed person, but I was not stupid. I just did not know how to say no to him. He had a large amount of confidence. I had a large amount of pride as well. I thought that he should have been more open in communication with me and that we should make some decisions as a couple. My quietness was probably misinterpreted by him as weakness. I went to Chicago with my sister, who was living with our older married sister. We became roommates there.

I soon found work in Chicago with the help of my nephew. My family in Chicago ensured that I would not be a financial burden on anyone. I got a job right away with a wholesale floorplan insurance company housed in the IBM Plaza on the 27th floor. Realistically an annual income of $8,000 back then was livable for me as I had no children, rent and board was $100 monthly. My only other bills were a car note and insurance. I was also able to shop for clothing and get my hair relaxed. I had gotten away from pressing and curling my hair when I switched to the afro at Tougaloo College.

I excelled on my job and within a year, I was promoted to Supervisor of Bookkeeping. I had one worker and a temporary working under me. Back then, jobs were relatively easy. The biggest challenge was getting to work. I lived on 100th Street and I would drive to 95th Street and ride the train to downtown, get off the train at the last stop near State Street and Wacker Drive. From there, I would walk across the bridge which crossed the Chicago River to the IBM Plaza where I worked on the 27th floor. One day as I was on break, I walked across the bridge and there I witnessed a man burning from spontaneous combustion right in front of my eyes. This was very unusual for me. There were other people around as well. Nobody panicked and I noticed that nobody called 911 before I left the scene. I did not want to believe that I had seen the man burn literally. This was the next most scary thing that I had seen for a while. The most scary thing was the movie, The Exorcist. I chose not to share this with the other employees back at the office as I was in such awe. I later researched and found that there is a such thing as spontaneous combustion. I learned from my research that most cases are not witnessed as I had. The incident took place about 10 feet away from me.

I am a loner, who has encountered several cases of impractical incidents, mostly dead bodies, over my lifetime. One of the incidents occurred in Chicago when I was out looking for a beauty supply store nearby a tavern. I looked on the sidewalk in South Chicago and observed that there was a dead body just outside the tavern, whose door was open, and many people were still sitting at the bar drinking and smoking. Nobody seemed to care that there was a murdered man on the sidewalk. I learned that I had adopted the philosophy that if a matter did not involve me, I would not invest my time nor have any input into the matter.

Back in the late 1960's when I saw the black man down during rush hour in Manhattan, New York as I was leaving work at The Federal Reserve, I was being carried by the crowd surging toward Grand Central Station, I wanted to call for help, but I could not. I rationalized that I could have been framed for murder as nobody else stopped to help. I just kept walking and buried the incident in my subconscious. These days, I would say that this is a sin of omission. But back then, I just shrugged it off. There were no cell phones in the 1960's.

I already gave an account of the woman, who was murdered in the tavern in Canton, Mississippi when I was traveling home from school from the Upward Bound Program, which was at Tougaloo College, near Jackson, MS. I suppressed that incident. Now when I reflect, I had decided that nobody cared, that nobody had time to be concerned as they were all busy handling their own problems and their business. I certainly felt that nobody cared had I gone to jail for a murder that I did not do. This was another case of rationalization and not seeing myself as the powerful teen that I was. Of course, many people saw good potential in me. Some idolized me. The rationalization was simply wrong having no basis. I was later to learn that I had a level of selfish pride. I only felt that I needed to survive by any means necessary.

When I moved to Los Angeles, California during the early 1980's, crack cocaine was becoming prevalent on the streets. One day when I was driving home from the health club, I drove upon a dead body on the sidewalk right by the stop sign at the corner of Hi Point and Western. This was remarkably close to my home. Rigor Mortis obviously had set in the dead body because he was perfectly stiff, lying on his back, eyes open and the sun was beaming on him. The body was a well-dressed African American Male. I had no problem driving away from the scene without panicking. I do not recall even mentioning the incident to my husband when he came home.

Sex is Over-rated, or is it?

I grew up in an era when everybody minded their own business. Unless you were invited to help by the person in need, the victim suffered. Nobody would check on a neighbor, who lived a mile away when she and her husband would have fights that could have been deadly. You could hear her screams a mile away. Yet nobody interfered. She never left the abuser, who sometimes resorted to using deadly weapons to quiet his jealous wife. One time he took an axe and hit her in the head. She did not die from the injury and later in the day when I was wandering, I witnessed the two of them making passionate love. There was no longer a need for any type of intervention. I made a mental note that this could have been this female's way of getting attention from her man, who was always working on cars in the front yard. Today, he was working on the car of another female that his wife was jealous of. The man was forced to hit the woman in the head and take her to bed to convince her that he loved her. She demonstrated the classical syndrome that abused women suffer from. They always go back to the lover as many as 23 times if they are not killed before number 23 comes up. The two of them lived together until death from natural causes.

I learned also from this couple that the woman is not always the victim. I hear men say that they were tricked by the woman. Well, I would suppose this statement to hold truth when she demands that the man removes the condom or refuse to use a condom because the feeling is so much better.

I have never used my difficulties in life as an excuse to not succeed. I just set goals and pursued them with rigor. This makes me realize that I was operating on autopilot most of my life. I did not realize that God's Favor was the true reason for my success. I just needed to couple my dreams with behaviors that would steer me to the results that I wanted to achieve. I unknowingly was doing something that many are not aware of. I was using my intuition and it was propelling me ahead.

I have noticed that I can become so immersed in the steps needed to accomplish what I set out to do that many times I have overlooked the fact that others are watching my behaviors. Over my lifetime, I was not aware on many occasions that others were using my life as a role model. My admirers did not know my story. Those who were challenging me because they thought that I had it made had no idea that I was hanging on by a string. Survival was a day-by-day ordeal. All that I can say at this stage of life is that I must apologize to any that I might have caused to stumble.

I truly was not aware that my actions could have any positive effect on the lives of others. I never looked at myself as being a star. And I certainly never wanted to be put on a pedestal because I believe that when you are raised up too high and you fall, the spiral downward is long and tormenting. Another disadvantage for me was that nobody dared to intervene and question my actions. Nobody pulled my coattail and told me that I needed to check myself. I think it would benefit anyone wanting to model their lives after another to refrain from having an interview with someone who has been raised up very highly by man. They would see that those elevated are surrounded by admirers, but more haters.

It took a long time for me to realize that the world did not revolve around me. I thought it savvy to be egotistical. I can see now that I really am a late bloomer. I also am aware that somebody has got to take the reins when there is no parental guidance, and in this case, it was me.

I believe that I have become so independent because I have had a lifelong problem with trust. When studying psychology, I learned that during childhood trust formation takes place between ages one to – three. In *psychology*, *trust* is believing that the person who is trusted will do what is expected. It starts at the family and grows to others. According to the Erikson theory of psychosocial *development*, developing basic *trust* is the infant *developmental* task occurring, or failing, during the first two years of life. The divorce occurred when I was two, just on the verge of becoming three years old. I am certain that the traumatic interference of parental separation during the trust formation stage of my life had much to do with my inability to allow others to get too close to me. At a certain point, I always put up a barrier.

You will not change unless you change the way you think. You will be the same twenty years later if you do not change your thinking. Changing your thinking is a process. Emotions, attitude, a decision to change course and the desire to excel were overwhelmingly a part of the process for me. I had faith that the course that I was on was the right way. I know now that faith works and that it is not just a religious term. Faith works in the secular realm as well just as it does in the spiritual realm.

I felt that I would achieve whatever I set out to achieve. I excelled in my endeavors. I campaigned to become High School Queen and the mission was accomplished. I kept my grades up in school and graduated co-valedictorian. I must have been attractive, I had dates. I achieved my Baccalaureate Degree in Psychology with a minor in Sociology. I married the man of my dreams at age 25. I received my Master of Social Work Degree. I was always able to keep myself gainfully employed until retirement.

I am just learning that there is a difference between opportunity and destiny. Opportunity is a one – time encounter while destiny is where we end up, no matter what. However, if one does not take advantage of his opportunities when they present, her destiny could be delayed.

I missed many good opportunities in life. It is puzzling that I cannot believe to this day that I allowed some of them to get by me.

I recall having walked away from jobs where I was being shown favor with the opportunity to be promoted. I cannot explain it. I attribute many of the missed opportunities to be because of my immaturity and my refusal to seek counseling from someone who I could trust. I was always leaning to my own understanding and trusted in myself.

I had read many books, but never wanted to read 'The Book'. If a book was not about romance, how to get rich quickly or comedy, I did not read it. I do recall religiously reading the Chicago Sun Times daily. I read the horoscope section first. I had subscriptions to fashion magazines, Newsweek, Time Life, but rarely picked up a bible.

God's Grace

The grace of God intervened, after years of stumbling and has taught me to bring my life into alignment with THE TRUTH, God's word. I have actually adopted and learned to apply the biblical verses, Prov. 3:5 & 6, "Trust in the Lord with all of your heart and lean not to your own understanding. Acknowledge Him in all of your ways and He will direct your paths" to my life.

I am so much better off and at peace with my life since I aligned my emotions, my thinking, and my appetites with THE TRUTH. I now know that truth is the highest realm of reality. I have learned to forgive myself for the many mistakes that I have made in this life now that I know that God has already forgiven me and sent his son Jesus to pay for my sin.

However, the road to getting to the point where I learned to lean on and trust in the Lord has been a long journey. I now use 'crazy faith' where my mind is not governed by what I can see, God propels me to another level once I have used up all my faith. Mark 2:11-12. Still, I trust God to see me through all tough situations. It is a daily walk, where I do not get anxious and panic when circumstances around me look grim. God continues to keep me. I have a peace that is unspeakable. I might sound arrogant to some, but I know who holds my future and I walk in the knowledge of knowing that God has my back.

Prologue

I continue to grow into my purpose, although I have not put a name on it. I continue to be stretched by studying, by life experiences that test my faith, and by the successes, failures, and the experiments that I test out of my curiosity.

I continue to dream. I am learning to use intuition as a tool to propel myself toward my land of plenty. I have learned to give up 'the need to know everything syndrome.' Not only have I learned to trust in God, but I have also learned to trust my intuition again.

I have grown to the point where I feel compelled to speak my mind, not having to censor what I am thinking because I have matured to the extent that my experience affects the outcome of my thoughts. I am determined to use faith-filled words when I speak because I know that faith-filled words will put me over. Fear-filled words will defeat me. I have learned over time that words are the most powerful things in the universe. God released faith with words. God created everything with faith-filled words. We are given the authority to bind and loose here on earth by speaking. Matthew 16:19. We determine what is established on the earth. Psalm 119:89.

Somewhere along the way I lost my childhood imagination, where I just enjoyed creating, not for financial gain. I just got a large amount of satisfaction from tapping into my talents and creating beautiful things. I spent a lot of time playing as a child and I am grateful for being allowed to do that by my family. To this day, I believe that certain traumas that have occurred in my life have eroded my freedom to imagine. I believe that the traumas have aborted my ability to imagine good and beautiful things because of the fear that too much imagination will cause a setback.

During the first developmental stage there must not be a break in the bond of attachment. The bond is severed when a child raised by consistently unreliable, unpredictable parents who do not meet this basic need. The child eventually develops an overall sense of mistrust. This is a good description of what happened to me. Mistrust can cause the child to become fearful, confused, and anxious, all of which make it difficult to form healthy relationships. This, in turn, can lead to poor social support, isolation, and loneliness.

Because babies are entirely dependent on their caregivers, it should come as no surprise that how parents interact with their babies has a profound effect on both their physical and mental health. I am not certain as to when Mama decided that she no longer wanted to be married to Daddy. However, I do know that she was always preoccupied and busy with chores around the house. There was no time for cuddling. I also learned from my sisters that when Mama came home with me, she practically turned me over to them to care for me.

In Freud's Theory, the second stage of psychosexual development is known as the anal stage. In this stage, children gain a sense of mastery and competence by controlling bladder and bowel movements. I had no problems with this stage. According to Freud's Theory, Children who succeed at this stage develop a sense of capability and productivity. Those who have problems at this stage may develop an anal fixation. As adults, they might be excessively orderly or messy.

Similarly, to Freud's Theory on the second stage, Erikson's Theory, Autonomy versus shame and doubt is the second stage of psychosocial development. During this stage, children become more mobile. They develop self-sufficiency by controlling activities such as eating, toilet training, and talking. Again, I had no problem with this stage in my life.

Both psychiatrist's theories are parallel on this stage: Children who are supported in this stage become more confident and independent. Those who are criticized or overly controlled are left doubting themselves.

I believe that Mama left Daddy at a good stage in my life because I was in this stage and ready to go to stage three.

As I continue to work toward self-improvement, I have learned to see patterns of regression and failure to reach goals and to create a bright future for myself. I am learning to recode when I find myself failing to be all that I want to be. Recoding keeps me from becoming a slave to doubt and the eight different ways that I can talk myself out of acting on my gut intuition. Gut intuition is far better for me than relying on my brain, my strength or my heart.

I just need to know what it is that I want to do and go for it. I have got to stop sabotaging myself by reacting, which creates what I do not want to do. I need to start being direct instead of dancing around the issue. Indirectness is like going to New Jersey by heading West. I cannot afford to do things based on what everyone else thinks. This kind of thinking is just a set up: I do not trust what I want and hold others hostage when my plan goes wrong. This kind of thinking is dependent on having to have a consensus. I have decided that I am powerful and will not default to letting the world choose for me. I have a blueprint for my life: The Holy Bible. I do not want to have a conditional control situation where I must compromise what I have for a more diluted situation. I must allow for expansion. I should not feel that I must have a safety net in my relationships. For example, I should not have to be in love with Johnny but have Edward in the wings just in case Johnny does not work out. I should just love Johnny. If Johnny does not love me back, I need to sever my relationship with Johnny or change the boundaries of our relationship. Then, I am free to start up a relationship with Edward if he is still available. No doubt there is another Johnny out there somewhere. I will not put limitations on what I want. I am not referring solely to romantic relationships here. If I decide that I want $8 billion, I will not compromise and say that I will settle for $5 billion. I will not wait for a universal sign to move forward. And I will resolve all negative beliefs about myself. I now see myself as God sees me: Blessed! My children are all grown and gone, happily married and no longer needing me to support them financially.

Justin and Joanna

Austin and Toneka